ARE YOU A GEEK?

10³ *ways to find out*

Tim Collins

DELTA TRADE PAPERBACKS

ARE YOU A GEEK?
A Delta Trade Paperback / September 2006

Published by
Bantam Dell
A Division of Random House, Inc.
New York, New York

Book design adapted by Robert Bull

Delta is a registered trademark of Random House, Inc., and the colophon is a
trademark of Random House, Inc.

Library of Congress Cataloging in Publication Data
Collins, Tim
  Are you a geek? : 10³ ways to find out / Tim Collins.
    p. cm.
  ISBN-13: 978-0-385-34015-1
  ISBN-10: 0-385-34015-X
  1. Geeks (Computer enthusiasts)–Humor. I. Title.

  PN6231.E4C65 2006
  004.02'07–dc22

                                    2006040289

Printed in the United States of America
Published simultaneously in Canada

www.bantamdell.com

BVG 10 9 8 7 6 5 4 3 2 1

You always read the copyright pages of books   ☐ **1 point**

Are You a Geek?
v1.0
by Tim Collins

Name: [   ]

Password: [   ]

(Log In)

Thanks to Collette Collins, Mike Hughes, Jim Derwent, Joe Cornish, Jake Lingwood, Claire Kingston, Emma Harrow, Julie Whelan, Rae Shirvington, Rachel Mills, Dan Newman, Alex Flint, Lawrence Hurley, Amanda Kolson Hurley, Holly Day, Danielle Perez and everyone at Ebury and Bantam Dell.

CONTENTS

ARE

YOU

A

GEEK?

INTRODUCTION

It's difficult to say exactly when it happened.

Maybe it was when everyone started getting web access at home. Maybe it was when *The Lord of the Rings* went to number one at the box office. Maybe it was when iPods became a fashion accessory.

I don't know exactly when, but at some point over the past few years, we all became a bit geekier.

It became all right for people in their twenties and thirties to buy console games. It became all right for adults to read children's books on trains. It became all right to email rather than phone.

But how do we know when we've gone too far with all of this?

How do we know when we've crossed the line from casual dabbler to genuine geek?

This book can help you find out.

Just check the boxes that apply to you as you read this book, add up your score, and fill out the appropriate certificate. Then cut it out and show it to your friends. If you have any.

If this book makes you realize that you're geekier than you thought, please don't try to hide it. Don't become one of those contact lens wearers who hide their consoles in drawers and sneak off to the bathroom for covert Tolkien breaks. You'll be much happier if you accept your true nature and come out of the geek closet right away.

Tim Collins
London, 2005

FAQS

I'm already pretty sure that I'm a geek.
Is it still worth taking this test?

Yes. In fact, if you think you've achieved an especially high score, email me at areyouageek@hotmail.co.uk and I'll tell you where you rank. But cheats beware—I might come around to your house to check that you've answered each section honestly. Except the "Sex" section.

I'm a girl. Can I take the test?

Yes. I'm well aware that, contrary to popular myth, many geeks these days are female. So, to make things fair, I've included a female version of the "Sex" section. Although you might have to stick to the male "Sex" section if you're a lesbian who has feelings about Gillian Anderson and Sarah Michelle Gellar.

I want to take the test but I don't want
to deface my new book. What should I do?

The best thing to do is buy two copies of the book—one to use and one to keep in mint condition. However, if you're a proper geek, you probably do this with every book you buy.

What's TARDIS an acronym for?

The "FYI" section at the back of the book should give you the answers to any such questions that occur while you're taking the test. FYI is an acronym for "For Your Information," in case you didn't know. And FAQs stands for "Frequently Asked Questions," in case you didn't even know that.

You live on your own. ☐ 1 point

You live with your mum. ☐ 2 points

...and you're over 30. ☐ 3 points

...and she still makes your meals, wakes you up in the morning, and checks your appearance before you leave the house. ☐ 5 points

You can't eat without watching TV at the same time. ☐ 1 point

You can't go to the bathroom without taking something to read with you. ☐ 1 point

You've got out of bed in the middle of the night because you couldn't resist checking your email. ☐ 2 points

While emptying your trash can, you've spotted litter that dated back more than 30 days. ☐ 1 point

If something goes wrong with your computer, you fix it right away, but if your washing machine breaks, you leave it for a while. ☐ 2 points

The last time you changed your sheets was over a month ago. ☐ 3 points

You have the following posters on your wall:

Data from Star Trek ☐ 1 point

Buffy ☐ 1 point

An Escher artwork ☐ 1 point

A map of the world ☐ 1 point

A magic eye picture ☐ 1 point

You've set aside an afternoon specifically to rearrange your CD collection. ☐ 3 points

You've set aside an evening specifically to watch the special features of a DVD. ☐ 3 points

You had a pizza delivered last night. ☐ 1 point

...and ate the cold remains of it for lunch today. ☐ 3 points

You've completed a takeout loyalty card in the last couple of weeks. ☐ 3 points

You often drink so much coffee or cola that you can't sleep at night. ☐ 2 points

When you can't sleep, you find yourself jotting down ideas for brilliant new inventions that make no sense in the morning. ☐ 3 points

You spend more on eBay than at your local supermarket. ☐ 3 points

ARE YOU A GEEK?

Look at the "call list" menu on your mobile and write down the last ten numbers you called.

1 ....

2 ....

3 ....

4 ....

5 ....

6 ....

7 ....

8 ....

9 ....

10 ....

Award yourself one point for every food delivery number you called.

◯ points

•BONUS POINTS•

Your personal smell can best be described as:

Axe   ☐ 1 point

Medicated soap   ☐ 2 points

Antiseptic cream   ☐ 3 points

Mildew   ☐ 4 points

A mixture of stale washing, secondhand books and piss   ☐ 5 points

---

You've actually done the following slapstick jokes in real life:

Walking into a lamppost because you were distracted by something   ☐ **1 point**

Slipping on a banana peel   ☐ **2 points**

Looking at your watch while holding a drink, and spilling it down yourself   ☐ **3 points**

Turning around suddenly while carrying a ladder, and hitting someone with it   ☐ **4 points**

Falling down an open manhole   ☐ **5 points**

Award yourself two points for every sex line you called.   ○ **points**

Award yourself five bonus points if you haven't called ten numbers yet.   ☐ **5 points**

You've drunk a soft drink straight from a 1.5 liter bottle to avoid washing a glass.   ☐ **3 points**

On the weekend, you always log in to your email before brushing your teeth.   ☐ **1 point**

You believe spraying yourself with deodorant is as good as showering.   ☐ **1 point**

You've had an argument with a roommate about whose turn it was to wash the dishes.   ☐ **1 point**

You've had an argument with a roommate about whose turn it was to phone for pizza.   ☐ **3 points**

You have a child.   ☐ **−1 point**

...but you spend more on toys and computer games than they do.

☐ 2 points

...and you've forced them to watch *Spirited Away* instead of the latest Disney animation.

☐ 3 points

You can drive.

☐ –1 point

...but you call your car "The Enterprise."

☐ 3 points

...and you say "Engage" when turning the ignition key.

☐ 5 points

...and you've given someone a detailed description of the engine.

☐ 5 points

You've used a computer today.

☐ 1 point

...and it's the weekend.

☐ 3 points

If your mouse breaks, you feel like you've had a limb amputated.

☐ 2 points

When your computer asks "Are you sure you want to shut down?" you actually think about it, and feel a bit guilty.

☐ 2 points

You've clicked on the option that tells you how long you've been playing a certain computer game for, and it was more than a week.

☐ 4 points

Before eating a package of M&Ms, you pour them out onto the table in front of you and arrange them according to color.

☐ 3 points

You actually quite enjoy the sensation of being addicted to a game and unable to put down the controller.

☐ 3 points

You often think of ways to complete day-to-day tasks slightly quicker, like adding milk to coffee while you're waiting for the water to boil, or flushing the toilet while you're still urinating.

☐ 1 point

You've considered moving to a larger property for the sake of a collection.

☐ 2 points

You feel strange if you go for longer than an hour without checking news headlines online, on your phone or on TV.

☐ 1 point

When doing your monthly budget, you put aside less than $10 for clothes and toiletries, and over $200 for entertainment and technology.

☐ 3 points

You actually do a monthly budget.

☐ 5 points

•BONUS POINTS•

You've arranged your CDs in the following order:

Alphabetical

☐ 1 point

Chronological (the order they were made)

☐ 2 points

Autobiographical (the order you bought them in)

☐ 3 points

In order of the color of their spines, to create a spectrum effect

☐ 4 points

In order of record label

☐ 5 points

ARE YOU A GEEK?

The bag you carry with you all the time is...

...an unbranded
rucksack worn by
both straps
☐ 1 point

...the same gym bag
you've had since
school and have
never washed
☐ 3 points

...a plastic bag from
a comic shop
on which the handles
are about to break
☐ 5 points

You've bought a Happy Meal or box of cereal
because it had a promotional gift licensed
from a sci-fi blockbuster.
☐ 1 point

You've bought something purely for its ironic value. ☐ 1 point

...which cost more than $60.
☐ 3 points

You've listed your religion as "Jedi"
when filling in a form.
☐ 1 point

You've eaten some Kendal Mint Cake.
☐ 1 point

You've changed an eating plan after being
unable to open a screw-topped jar.
☐ 1 point

You've decided to stay in after being unable
to find one of your shoes.
☐ 1 point

You celebrate Halloween more than your
own birthday.
☐ 3 points

You've tripped over the following things:

A high curb — 1 point

A loose paving stone — 3 points

Your own feet — 5 points

You've taken an elevator to travel one floor, which took longer than walking would have done. — 1 point

You're the only person in your office who hasn't gotten their kids to record their answering-machine message. — 1 point

That's because you rerecord your answering-machine message every day, giving a detailed description of your schedule for that day. — 3 points

You've been to a midnight opening of a shop when a book, DVD or game was released. — 1 point

You've set up your computer so that you can watch TV at the same time as playing games. — 1 point

There are more TVs than rooms in your house. — 1 point

...and you keep all of them on all the time. — 3 points

When watching TV, you close the curtains, turn the lights off and sit about three inches away from the screen. — 3 points

You feel powerless when someone else in the room is holding the remote control. — 1 point

ARE YOU A GEEK?

In winter, you often get that horrible feeling when it gets dark outside and you realize you haven't left the house yet.

☐ 1 point

In summer, you often get that horrible feeling when it gets dark outside and you realize you haven't left the house yet.

☐ 3 points

You're so used to having the curtains closed in summer that it takes you a while to get used to the bright sunshine when you finally leave the house.

☐ 1 point

You own a thermos bottle.

☐ 3 points

You own a clock that displays all the world time zones.

☐ 1 point

•BONUS POINTS•

For you, getting ready to leave the house in the morning means...

...showering, shaving, ironing your shirt and trousers, brushing your teeth, combing your hair, applying deodorant, dressing, leaving the house.

☐ 1 point

...washing your armpits over the sink, brushing your teeth, putting on clean clothes, leaving the house.

☐ 2 points

...searching for the cleanest pair of pants on your floor, putting on the same clothes as the previous day, leaving the house.

☐ 3 points

...getting out of bed, leaving the house in the clothes you slept in.

☐ 5 points

Your watch has the following features:

Hourly chime ☐ 1 point

Calculator ☐ 1 point

Compass ☐ 1 point

Multiple time zones ☐ 1 point

Waterproof to 200 yards ☐ 1 point

You bought it so you knew when you could start playing against your trans-Atlantic cyber friends online. ☐ 3 points

You follow instructions even if they're clearly just there as a legal mandatory, like checking with your doctor before using your exercise bike. ☐ 1 point

You've had a nightmare about your Nintendo DS, iPod and portable DVD player all running out of batteries at the same time on a long journey. ☐ 1 point

You know the exact amount of sleep you need to get by and you complain about being tired for the entire following day if you get slightly less. ☐ 1 point

Every single plug in your house has a power strip attached to it. ☐ 2 points

Your dog is called "Chewie." ☐ 3 points

You have a filing cabinet in your house. ☐ 2 points

ARE YOU A GEEK?

The only time you ever shower is when
you're itching so much it gets in the way
of your game playing.

☐ 4 points

You have more than five allergies.

☐ 2 points

...and one of them is for soap.

☐ 4 points

You've scanned or photocopied a part of yourself.

☐ 1 point

The technology inside your house
is worth more than the house itself.

☐ 4 points

You registered your name as a dot com domain
back in 1994, so now the lawyer in Philadelphia
with the same name as you has to use dot net for
his site, even though he attracts five thousand
times more traffic than you.

☐ 5 points

You often get nosebleeds for no apparent reason.

☐ 1 point

You always keep your books in perfect order,
but you don't mind leaving all your clothes
in a pile in front of your closet.

☐ 1 point

You've looked at your watch and realized that your role-playing games session has passed the 12-hour mark.

☐ **3 points**

You've looked at your watch and realized that your role-playing games session has passed the 24-hour mark.

☐ **5 points**

You've spent more than an hour thinking about the meaning of existence.

☐ **1 point**

You weren't lying awake at night with insomnia at the time.

☐ **3 points**

You still try to avoid stepping on the cracks between paving stones.

☐ **5 points**

You've had a dream that you believed to be a message sent to you by a powerful sage, instructing you to go on a quest.

☐ **5 points**

You have more food delivery menus pinned to your fridge than items of food inside it.

☐ **2 points**

You measure time in how many episodes of *Buffy* you could have watched.

☐ **1 point**

You have over ten different types of power adaptors in your house (add a point for each additional type).

◯ **points**

You've taken a day off work on the day a book by your favorite author was released.

☐ **3 points**

You've taken a day off work for an astronomical event.

☐ **5 points**

You've bought your own pencil sharpener, stapler, calculator or hole punch, just so you could have the best one in the office.

☐ **3 points**

　　　　　　　　ARE YOU A GEEK?

You've devised a contingency plan for the following eventualities:

A virus turning most of the population into flesh-eating zombies ☐ 1 point

A virus killing most of the population, leaving the survivors to rebuild society ☐ 1 point

Hostile alien attack ☐ 1 point

Plants or animals turning hostile and trying to wipe out the human race ☐ 1 point

Nuclear war ☐ 1 point

You've stuck action figures to your computer at work. ☐ 2 points

You've taken responsibility for the alarm system at every office you've ever worked in, as you're always the first to get in and the last to leave. ☐ 4 points

You've been mentioned briefly in a trade magazine, and sent a photocopy of the article to everyone you know. ☐ 4 points

You work in an IT department. ☐ 4 points

...and you've thought to yourself, "I can't believe they're paying me to do this," while installing a motherboard. ☐ 5 points

...and you've asked someone "How long is a piece of string?" when they wanted to know how long it would take you to fix their computer. ☐ 5 points

...and you've asked someone "Which part of the sentence 'I'm too busy to do it at the moment' don't you understand?"

☐ 5 points

You work in a comic shop.

☐ 3 points

You don't work in a comic shop, but you spend all your time hanging around in one anyway.

☐ 4 points

When there's a signing on at your local comic shop, you always turn up early so you can make new friends in the line.

☐ 5 points

IF YOU'RE ANGRY WITH SOMEONE AT WORK, YOU SEND THEM AN EMAIL IN UPPER CASE.

☐ 1 POINT

You've eaten cereal out of a measuring cup because you couldn't be bothered to wash a bowl.

☐ 2 points

Your mobile ring tone is the *Doctor Who* theme, "The Imperial March," or a recording of yourself shouting "Ring Ring! Pick up your phone!"

☐ 1 point

Your password is "Lothlórien" or "Rivendell."

☐ 1 point

Your PIN is 1138.

☐ 1 point

If you're really angry with someone at work, you change their screen saver to some porn.

☐ 3 points

If you're *really* angry with someone at work, you sign up their email address for spam.

☐ 5 points

You've fantasized about being a rock star.

☐ 1 point

You've fantasized about having superpowers.

☐ 3 points

You've fantasized about solving a difficult equation. ☐ 5 points

ARE YOU A GEEK?

To you, a "marathon" means watching all the extended editions of *The Lord of the Rings* without stopping, rather than running 26 miles without stopping.

☐ 1 point

You've never answered "No" to the question "Continue?"

☐ 1 point

Total points for this section:

You've been called any of the following names:

Egghead	☐ 1 point	Four Eyes	☐ 1 point	
Brainiac	☐ 1 point	Techie	☐ 1 point	
Whiz Kid	☐ 1 point	Propeller Head	☐ 1 point	
Bookworm	☐ 1 point	Loser	☐ 1 point	
Hacker	☐ 1 point	Dungeon Master	☐ 1 point	
Poindexter	☐ 1 point	Brains	☐ 1 point	
Dork	☐ 1 point	Fanboy	☐ 1 point	
Dweeb	☐ 1 point	Technocrat	☐ 1 point	
Professor	☐ 1 point	AV Guy	☐ 1 point	
Square	☐ 1 point		
Dorkwad	☐ 1 point	**Total**	◯ points

ARE YOU A GEEK?

You own a T-shirt with the logo of a computer firm on it.

☐ **1 point**

You own a T-shirt with the name of your school chess team on it.

☐ **3 points**

You own a T-shirt with a picture of yourself at a fan convention on it.

☐ **5 points**

You've worn a T-shirt for more than five days running (add one point for each additional day).

◯ **points**

You've worn a pair of underpants for more than five days running (add two points for each additional day).

◯ **points**

You find that people tend to stand rather than sit next to you, even on a very crowded bus.

☐ **3 points**

You've worn a style of clothing for so long that it came back into fashion as "retro" and "ironic."

☐ **1 point**

You've worn a shirt with one collar tucked into your sweater and the other sticking out.

☐ **1 point**

You've worn clothes that were still slightly damp from being washed.

☐ 1 point

You've worn an item of clothing inside out by mistake.

☐ 2 points

You've worn the waistband of your trousers really high with your shirt tucked in.

☐ 3 points

You've worn a fluorescent safety strip while cycling. ☐ 2 points

You've worn a fluorescent safety strip while walking at night.

☐ 3 points

You've worn orthopedic shoes.

☐ 3 points

You've worn combat gear.

☐ 3 points

You've worn a bow tie.

☐ 4 points

• BONUS POINTS •

The celebrity you most closely resemble is...

Kevin Smith

☐ 1 point

Rick Moranis

☐ 2 points

Bill Gates c.1978

☐ 3 points

Clay Aiken from American Idol

☐ 4 points

Stephen Hawking

☐ 5 points

ARE YOU A GEEK?

You have any of the following types of facial hair:

Downy moustache ☐ 1 point if male

☐ 2 points if female

Stubble (unintentional) ☐ 2 points

Goatee ☐ 3 points

Pointed beard ☐ 4 points

Beard with no moustache ☐ 5 points

You've worn a cloak. ☐ 4 points

You've worn sandals and socks. ☐ 4 points

You've worn a mobile phone holster. ☐ 4 points

You've worn a scientific calculator holster. ☐ 5 points

You've worn a fanny pack. ☐ 5 points

...and you weren't on vacation at the time. ☐ 5 points

You bought a can of Axe last summer, and you haven't used it all yet. ☐ 1 point

Your coat has more than two pockets (add a point for each additional pocket). ◯ points

You often get trapped in that situation where you get stuck in the way of someone walking toward you, and you both move the same way to try and get past.

1 point

You have bad breath (get someone else to check this if you can't tell).

1 point

You have a weight problem.

1 point

...that you've blamed on a rare glandular disorder...

3 points

...while eating a stuffed-crust pizza.

5 points

Your glasses are thicker than this book.

1 point

Your glasses are thicker than *The Hitchhiker's Guide to the Galaxy*.

3 points

Your glasses are thicker than *The Lord of the Rings*.

5 points

You believe that hair washes itself if you leave it alone.

1 point

•BONUS POINTS•

The place you most frequently buy clothes from is...

The military surplus store

1 point

Forbidden Planet

3 points

eBay

5 points

ARE YOU A GEEK?

You believe that clothes iron themselves if you wear them. ☐ **2 points**

You believe that spraying your clothes with Axe is as good as putting them in the washing machine. ☐ **1 point**

If your glasses slip down your nose, you shove them back up by pushing the bridge with your index finger. ☐ **1 point**

You've never knowingly been color coordinated. ☐ **1 point**

Check the clothes you are currently wearing for food stains and draw them on the diagram below.

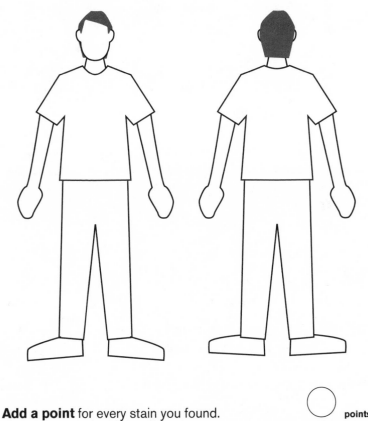

Add a point for every stain you found. ◯ **points**

• BONUS POINTS •

You have the following tattoos:

An infinity symbol ☐ 1 point

A bar code ☐ 2 points

An Atari logo ☐ 3 points

A DNA helix ☐ 4 points

*A tattoo of Sarah Michelle Gellar's face
that covers your entire back* ☐ 5 points

As a child, you wore a school blazer. ☐ 1 point

...even though it was an optional part
of the uniform. ☐ 3 points

...even though it was the weekend. ☐ 5 points

You keep a used tissue stuffed up your
sleeve at all times. ☐ 1 point

You have a sniffle all year round. ☐ 1 point

You've burned off more calories buying sportswear
than you ever have playing sports. ☐ 1 point

You've bought an item of clothing because you
thought it wouldn't show stains easily. ☐ 3 points

You own less than four pairs of trousers. ☐ 1 point

...and none of them are quite long enough for you. ☐ 3 points

ARE YOU A GEEK?

When deciding which clothes to wear,
you often have to smell several items to decide
which is least dirty.

☐ 1 point

The nearest you've gotten to wearing a suit is
putting a smart jacket on over the top of your
Babylon 5 T-shirt.

☐ 1 point

You keep your mouth open when concentrating.

☐ 2 points

Every time you try to go clothes shopping,
you find yourself spending all your time in Tower,
Sam Goody or Radio Shack instead.

☐ 1 point

You believe that the *Star Wars* character you most
closely resemble is Han Solo.

☐ 1 point

Most people believe that the *Star Wars* character
you most closely resemble is Jabba the Hut.

☐ 3 points

You've grown a beard to avoid shaving in the
morning, so you can stay in bed slightly longer.

☐ 1 point

You've spent more than $40 on a comic,
but never more than $20 on a shirt.

☐ 3 points

You only replace your clothes when they're
so old that they rip when you try to put them on.

☐ 1 point

You suspect Jehovah's Witnesses make a
beeline for you when they're handing out leaflets,
as you look like an easy target.

☐ 4 points

To you, a mirror is a website that mimics the URL
of another one rather than something you glance
at to check your physical appearance.

☐ 3 points

You've cut your own hair.

☐ 1 point

...without looking in a mirror.

☐ 3 points

STYLE

You have greasy hair. ☐ **1 point**

You had to feel your hair before ticking the last box, as you have no awareness whatsoever of your physical appearance. ☐ **4 points**

You often buy clothes because they're made from a scientifically innovative fabric, rather than because they're fashionable. ☐ **3 points**

You currently have an instruction such as "buy toilet paper" written on your hand in pen. ☐ **1 point**

You change your desktop picture more often than your socks. ☐ **3 points**

You've actually used those clips you get on the back of mobile phone, iPod and BlackBerry carrying cases that let you attach them to your belt. ☐ **3 points**

The sartorial disaster you fear most is showing up for the pub quiz wearing the same *Red Dwarf* T-shirt as the team captain. ☐ **1 point**

You dread going to the hairdresser as much as going to the dentist. ☐ **1 point**

You check your email more frequently than your physical appearance. ☐ **1 point**

ARE YOU A GEEK?

Total points for this section:

Total points so far:

• BONUS CHECKLIST •

You've seen the following films (one point for each time you've seen them):

Star Wars *Episodes I, II, III, IV, V and VI*	points	*Every Kevin Smith movie*	points
Every Star Trek *movie*	points	*Every Roger Corman movie*	points
Every Marvel comic adaptation	points	*Every Quentin Tarantino movie*	points
Minority Report	points	*Every Tim Burton movie*	points
Bladerunner	points	*Every Ed Wood movie*	points
2001: A Space Odyssey	points	*All the* Indiana Jones *films*	points
Forbidden Planet	points	*All the* Back to the Future *trilogy*	points
The Alien *films*	points	*All of* The Matrix *trilogy*	points
Pi	points	*All of* The Lord of the Rings *trilogy*	points
Jacob's Ladder	points		
War Games	points	**Total**	points

● S O C I A L

L I F E ●

The last night out you had was over a week ago. ☐ 1 point

The last night out you had was over a month ago. ☐ 3 points

The last night out you had was over a year ago. ☐ 5 points

You've been the first person to show up at a party. ☐ 1 point

You've been the only person to show up at a party. ☐ 3 points

You've been to a party that you thought you had
the wrong address for, as there was so little noise
coming from inside the house. ☐ 3 points

At the last party you went to, more than three
people told you they were just popping off to
get a drink and didn't return. ☐ 3 points

You sometimes get the impression that everyone's
waiting for you to leave the party so it can get
going properly. ☐ 5 points

At the last party you went to, you were disappointed
that the Java programmers and the C++
programmers didn't mingle. ☐ 5 points

You've seen someone's eyes darting around the room in panic to look for someone else to talk to, while you were telling them that Venus is the only planet that rotates clockwise.

☐ 5 points

You've deliberately made friends with someone geekier than you so you could look cool by comparison.

☐ 3 points

You've phoned someone specifically to gloat about beating them at Trivial Pursuit.

☐ 3 points

Someone has phoned you to get you to talk them through setting the timer on their video or DVD recorder.

☐ 1 point

You've arranged to meet someone at a really specific time, like 11:47, because you've worked out exactly how long it would take you to get somewhere.

☐ 1 point

If someone tells you to give them a minute, you time out exactly 60 seconds on your watch.

☐ 1 point

You've missed an important social engagement because there was a *Quantum Leap* marathon on the Sci-Fi Channel, and it's not the same if you record it and watch it later.

☐ 2 points

You spent your last birthday on your own.

☐ 3 points

You spent last New Year's Eve on your own.

☐ 5 points

When greeting someone, you try to avoid hugging or kissing them.

☐ 1 point

When greeting someone, you try to avoid shaking hands with them.

☐ 3 points

When greeting someone, you try to avoid looking at them or saying "Hello."

☐ 5 points

You've been to a fast-food restaurant on your own.

☐ 1 point

You've been to a cinema on your own.

☐ 2 points

You've been to a heavy rock concert on your own.

☐ 3 points

You've been to a pub on your own.

☐ 4 points

You've been to a fan convention on your own.

☐ 5 points

You spent all day at the convention in the video room, as you were too scared to go out and talk to new people.

☐ 5 points

You've sent yourself an email.

☐ 1 point

You've left yourself a voice message.

☐ 1 point

ARE YOU A GEEK?

You've boycotted a social engagement because the clip art on the invitation was so outmoded.

☐ *3 points*

When you lived in a dorm at college, you'd often ask the people in the room next door to be quiet, so you could get on with your studies.

☐ 1 point

You would do this even on a Friday night.

☐ 3 points

You've played a drinking game based on a film or TV show, such as *Star Trek*, *The X-Files* or *Babylon 5*.

☐ 2 points

You were alone at the time.

☐ 5 points

You have less than 30 friends.

☐ 1 point

You have less than 20 friends.

☐ 2 points

You have less than 10 friends.

☐ 3 points

You have less than 10 friends, including people you have only ever communicated with by email.

☐ 4 points

SOCIAL LIFE

You have less than 10 friends, including your Sims. □ 5 points

You've attempted to measure your alcohol tolerance by getting drunk and writing down a description of your mental state. □ 5 points

Someone has assumed you're gay because they've never seen you with any members of the opposite sex. □ 1 point

You've struck up a conversation with someone because they were a fellow early adopter (for example, someone else who had the white iPod earbuds a couple of years ago). □ 1 point

You usually check the TV guide before deciding whether to go out or not. □ 1 point

Amount of alcohol	Strength of alcohol	Time	Description of mental state — e.g. happy, depressed
1 pint			
2 pints			
3 pints			
4 pints			
5 pints			
6 pints			
7 pints			
8 pints			
9 pints			
10 pints			

ARE YOU A GEEK?

You've been to a party where the following happened:

Everybody played charades ☐ **1 point**

Everybody left before midnight ☐ **2 points**

Someone referred to wine as "el vino" ☐ **3 points**

No girls turned up ☐ **4 points**

Everyone solved logic puzzles ☐ **5 points**

When someone accuses you of being boring, you respond with a long and rambling monologue listing reasons why you're actually quite interesting. ☐ **2 points**

You've been the only person who didn't dance at a wedding, nightclub or concert. ☐ **1 point**

You've pretended to have a headache so you could leave a social engagement to go home and read. ☐ **2 points**

You've waited until after a TV show to return someone's call. ☐ **1 point**

You've given up on a conversation with someone because they confused *Star Trek* with *Star Wars*. ☐ **1 point**

You've given up on a conversation with someone because they confused Sauron and Saruman. ☐ **2 points**

Less than half the people in your office know who you are. ☐ **1 point**

SOCIAL LIFE

...and less than 50 people work there.

☐ 3 points

The vast majority of people in your office only talk to you when they're thinking of buying a computer and want some advice.

☐ 3 points

The only time everyone at work notices that you've gone on vacation is when the printer jams and they need someone to fix it.

☐ 4 points

You've cut out a newspaper headline that contained the name of one of your colleagues and stuck it on the bulletin board.

☐ 1 point

You've written a limerick about a work colleague.

☐ 1 point

...and read it out loud at their birthday drinks.

☐ 3 points

The only time the best-looking woman in your office spoke to you was when she couldn't work out how to underline text in Word.

☐ 1 point

You tried to start a conversation about this with her at the Christmas party.

☐ 3 points

In your last birthday card from work, more than 10 people wrote "Have a good one," because they've never spoken to you.

☐ 1 point

A work colleague has invited you to their house on a Saturday.

☐ −1 point

...but it was because they wanted their new PC set up.

☐ 5 points

The second controller you got as part of your PlayStation 2 package has never been used.

☐ 3 points

ARE YOU A GEEK?

You've deliberately lent something to someone at work so you'd have an excuse to go back over and talk to them later.

☐ 4 points

At your last office party, you found yourself standing in a group consisting of the IT guy, an accountant and the night watchman.

☐ 2 points

If someone from your office throws a party, you tend to find out about it the day after it happens.

☐ 2 points

To you, "networking" means connecting all the computers in your office together, rather than meeting people who could help your career.

☐ 1 point

You're reading this book on a Friday or Saturday night.

☐ 2 points

You were given this book as a gift in your office "Secret Santa."

☐ 5 points

•BONUS POINTS•

When watching a DVD at a friend's house, you complain if anyone...

...speaks

☐ 1 point

...walks in front of the TV

☐ 2 points

...eats

☐ 3 points

...breathes loudly

☐ 4 points

...moves in any way

☐ 5 points

Total points for this section:

Total points so far:

•BONUS CHECKLIST•

You've watched a full episode of the following TV shows:

Doctor Who	☐ 1 point	Star Trek: Deep Space Nine	☐ 1 point	
Blake's Seven	☐ 1 point	Star Trek: Voyager	☐ 1 point	
Farscape	☐ 1 point	Star Trek: Enterprise	☐ 1 point	
Battlestar Galactica	☐ 1 point	Babylon 5	☐ 1 point	
Xena	☐ 1 point	The X-Files	☐ 1 point	
The Prisoner	☐ 1 point	Quantum Leap	☐ 1 point	
Firefly	☐ 1 point	The Twilight Zone	☐ 1 point	
The Avengers	☐ 1 point	Twin Peaks	☐ 1 point	
Buffy the Vampire Slayer	☐ 1 point	Transformers	☐ 1 point	
Star Trek	☐ 1 point			
Star Trek: The Next Generation	☐ 1 point	**Total**	◯ points	

ARE YOU A GEEK?

You own an iPod (add one point per gigabyte). ◯ **points**

You are currently listening to it (add two points per gigabyte). ◯ **points**

You often listen to it and play your portable gaming system at the same time (add three points per gigabyte). ◯ **points**

You often sing along to it while in public (add four points per gigabyte). ◯ **points**

You have an Iron Maiden track stored on it (add five points per gigabyte). ◯ **points**

You've downloaded more songs than you've ever bought on CD. ☐ **3 points**

You've spoiled a concert for someone else by loudly singing along to the lyrics. ☐ **1 point**

You've kept the ticket stub for every concert you've ever been to. ☐ **3 points**

You've created experimental electronic music on your computer. ☐ **3 points**

You've pretended to your friends that you were offered a record contract to release it, but you turned it down because you were already earning so much from working in IT.

☐ 5 points

You always try to get into bands that are more obscure than the ones your friends are into.

☐ 1 point

You always "christen" a new stereo with one of your favorite albums, so you'll remember which song you played on it first.

☐ 3 points

You've been through a phase of getting into classic rock bands from the past and telling all your friends how much today's bands have stolen from them.

☐ 1 point

You've memorized the lyrics of your favorite album.

☐ 3 points

•BONUS POINTS•

You were the only person in the cinema who laughed at the following movie in-jokes...

When we see that the club in Indiana Jones and the Temple of Doom *is called "Obi Wan."*

☐ 1 point

When Ash has to learn the words "Klaatu," "Barada," "Nikto" in Evil Dead 3: Army of Darkness, *which are the same words that are used to command Gort in* The Day the Earth Stood Still.

☐ 3 points

When we see that the cinema in Back to the Future *is playing a double bill of* A Boy's Life *and* Watch the Skies—*the working titles for* ET *and* Close Encounters of the Third Kind.

☐ 5 points

ARE YOU A GEEK?

You've memorized the catalog number of your favorite album. □ **5 points**

You've listened to a song with a really long guitar solo (add a point for each minute the solo lasted). ○ **points**

You've burned a CD for friends that included extensive liner notes you wrote yourself. □ **3 points**

You've bought a CD because it was right for your collection rather than because you really wanted to listen to it. □ **5 points**

You own a movie sound track CD. □ **1 point**

You own a TV show sound track CD. □ **3 points**

You own a video game sound track CD. □ **5 points**

You've watched *The Wizard of Oz* while listening to *Dark Side of the Moon* to see if it's true that it spookily matches up. □ **1 point**

You've watched the same film twice in one day. □ **3 points**

...it was *The Last Starfighter.* □ **5 points**

You've stayed in a cinema until after the credits, in case there was an extra bit at the end. □ **1 point**

You've moved seats in the middle of a film to get away from someone who was eating popcorn too loudly. □ **2 points**

You tend to go to the cinema in the daytime, when it's less likely to be full of noisy people. □ **2 points**

You have a favorite seat in your local cinema, and you always get there early to make sure no one else is sitting in it. □ **2 points**

You've been annoyed by the following song lyrics:

The bit in "Champagne Supernova" by Oasis where Liam claims to be slowly walking down a hall faster than a cannonball. Which would either mean that the cannonball was traveling very slowly or was completely stationary. □ 1 point

The bit in "Should I Stay or Should I Go?" by The Clash, in which Joe Strummer states that if he goes there will be trouble but if he stays there will be double, which means that he should clearly go, rendering the question redundant. □ 1 point

The bit in "Killer Queen" where Freddie Mercury states that the killer queen never kept the same address to avoid complication, whereas surely this would increase complication. □ 1 point

The bit in "Tonight" by New Kids on the Block where they claim to have traveled round the world and met a lot of people and girls. □ 1 point

The entire lyrics to "Ironic" by Alanis Morissette, which list a number of things that aren't actually ironic, like it raining on your wedding day. □ 1 point

You've told someone in a cinema to stop talking. □ 3 points

The person in question was a child you were sitting next to in the last Pixar movie. □ 5 points

You own a pen with a light on the end. □ 1 point

You bought it so you could make a note of any continuity errors you spotted while in the cinema. □ 3 points

You've watched a rereleased film in the cinema. □ 1 point

...and got angry when the audience laughed at the dated special effects.

☐ 3 points

You've gone to the cinema dressed as a character from the film.

☐ 3 points

...the film in question was a serious drama rather than a sci-fi movie.

☐ 5 points

You've refused to watch a film because it was a "pan and scan" rather than widescreen version.

☐ 1 point

You've refused to watch a film because it was dubbed.

☐ 3 points

...the film in question was animated.

☐ 5 points

You've interrupted someone who was about to rent a DVD from Blockbuster to warn them about how bad it is.

☐ 1 point

You've been to see a film because of the director, rather than the star.

☐ 1 point

You've been to see a film because of the director of photography.

☐ 3 points

You've been to see a film because of the director of visual effects.

☐ 5 points

You've seen your favorite film > ten times.

☐ 3 points

You automatically read > as "more than" in the above sentence.

☐ 5 points

You've spoiled a film for the people you were watching it with by correctly predicting the ending.

☐ 3 points

You've spoiled a film for the people you were watching it with by explaining why an action sequence is scientifically impossible.

☐ 3 points

You've spoiled a high school sex comedy for the people you were watching it with by pointing out that all the actors in it are far too old to still be in school.

☐ 3 points

You've spoiled a crime movie for the people you were watching it with by pointing out how unlikely it is that a news report about the criminals would start exactly as they turn their TV on.

☐ 3 points

You'd rather watch a sci-fi B-movie than an Oscar winner.

☐ 1 point

...unless it won for best visual effects.

☐ 1 point

...or unless it was *The Return of the King*. Obviously.

☐ 1 point

If you're a big fan of a movie, you refuse to admit to yourself that the sequel is rubbish.

☐ 1 point

•BONUS POINTS•

You've said to someone, "I can't believe you've never seen that film!" with reference to the following:

The Godfather

☐ 1 point

The Goonies

☐ 2 points

Soylent Green

☐ 3 points

Krull

☐ 4 points

The Lawnmower Man 2: Beyond Cyberspace

☐ 5 points

ARE YOU A GEEK?

You've tried to replicate a special move from a beat-'em-up game in a real fight.

☐ 1 point

You've bought a DVD with three separate commentaries, and listened to them one after the other as soon as you got home.

☐ 3 points

You've never watched the critically acclaimed art-house DVD you keep on your shelf next to your copy of *Battlestar Galactica*.

☐ 3 points

You've spent so long choosing a DVD from your huge collection that you didn't have enough time left to watch it.

☐ 3 points

If someone buys you a movie on VHS instead of DVD, you find it hard to pretend to be pleased.

☐ 1 point

You keep all the receipts of the DVDs you buy.

☐ 1 point

...this isn't so you can declare them on your tax return, but because you're so proud that you bought them on the day they came out.

☐ 3 points

You've bought a "special edition" DVD of a film you already own.

☐ 3 points

You buy every horror movie that gets released on DVD, even if it's *Stigmata, House of the Dead* or *Blair Witch 2: Book of Shadows*.

☐ 3 points

You refused to tick the above box because you prefer the term "dark fantasy" to "horror."

☐ 4 points

You buy every sci-fi movie that gets released on DVD, even if it's *Pluto Nash, Battlefield Earth* or *Mission to Mars*.

☐ 3 points

You keep a notebook to jot down ideas for sci-fi movies.

☐ 4 points

ENTERTAINMENT

You've convinced yourself that the writers of a new sci-fi blockbuster somehow stole the idea from your notebook.

☐ 5 points

You've watched all the *Star Wars* films back to back.

☐ 3 points

...alone.

☐ 5 points

You've written to George Lucas, suggesting story ideas for episodes VII–IX and offering to direct.

☐ 1 point

You are boycotting the *Star Wars* trilogy on DVD until they release the original theatrical versions.

☐ 1 point

You've watched a movie that featured a heavy metal title track over the closing credits.

☐ 3 points

You own a PS2, an Xbox 360 or a GameCube.

☐ 1 point

You own a PS2, an Xbox 360 *and* a GameCube.

☐ 3 points

...and you've bought the same game for all three consoles to see if there were any differences.

☐ 5 points

You've moved your console controller violently to the side you want your car to go while playing a driving game.

☐ 1 point

You've imagined a John Madden–style commentary on your performance while playing a computer game.

☐ 2 points

You've had a console chipped so you could buy import games and finish them a few weeks before anyone else.

☐ 2 points

You've had a "console hangover" from staying up really late to finish a game on a work night.

☐ 3 points

ARE YOU A GEEK?

You've searched for the following things in movies:

The ghost of a dead boy that appears at the window in Three Men and a Baby. ☐ **1 point**

The Munchkin suicide in The Wizard of Oz. ☐ **1 point**

The bit in Star Wars *where a Stormtrooper accidentally hits his head.* ☐ **1 point**

The bit where the word "sex" appears in the dust in The Lion King, *which was added by a disgruntled animator.* ☐ **1 point**

The scene in The Crow *where Brandon Lee is killed on-screen.* ☐ **1 point**

Award yourself a bonus point if you believe that both Bruce Lee and Brandon Lee were killed by the Chinese mafia for revealing secret martial arts techniques on film. ☐ **1 point**

You've upgraded a computer for the sake of a new game. ☐ **2 points**

You pray that you live long enough to see actual photo-realism in games. ☐ **1 point**

You've justified a lengthy computer game session to yourself on the grounds that it improves your hand-eye coordination, even though the only thing you ever do that requires hand-eye coordination is playing computer games. ☐ **2 points**

You've bought a computer game on the day it came out. ☐ **2 points**

You've bought an operating system on the day it came out. ☐ **3 points**

ENTERTAINMENT

You've felt exhausted after spending a weekend unlocking characters in a beat-'em-up game.

☐ 2 points

...and you actually felt like you'd achieved something.

☐ 3 points

You've been thrown out of an arcade for spending too long on the games without losing a life.

☐ 3 points

You have a drawer full of Atari 2500 cartridges you can't bring yourself to throw away.

☐ 3 points

You convinced your parents to buy you a home computer on the grounds that you would use it to learn programming rather than just play games.

☐ 3 points

You actually did use it to learn programming.

☐ 5 points

•BONUS POINTS•

Your taste in music could best be described as...

...Jessica Simpson, Britney Spears, Christina Aguilera

☐ – 1 point

...Coldplay, Radiohead, Keane

☐ 1 point

...Pink Floyd, Rush, Yes

☐ 2 points

...Metallica, Slayer, Megadeth

☐ 3 points

...Weezer, They Might Be Giants, Devo

☐ 4 points

...William Shatner

☐ 5 points

ARE YOU A GEEK?

You've played a computer game for so long that you couldn't move your thumbs. ☐ 3 points

You've played a computer game for so long that you could see it when you closed your eyes. ☐ 4 points

You've played a violent first-person computer game for so long that you imagined killing passers-by while walking down the street. ☐ 5 points

You've played a violent first-person computer game for so long that you actually did kill passers-by while walking down the street (add a point for every victim). ○ points

You've been to an author signing event. ☐ 1 point

You've asked a question at an author signing event. ☐ 3 points

...which was about an inaccuracy or inconsistency that you'd noticed in one of their books. ☐ 5 points

You've bought a book you already own because it was reissued with a new cover. ☐ 2 points

You've annoyed people in your train car by exclaiming loudly upon noticing that the name of one of the characters in your book is an anagram of the villain's name. ☐ 3 points

You've annoyed people in your train by snorting with laughter at a Terry Pratchett novel. ☐ 3 points

You then annoyed them even more by muttering to yourself, "Genius, thy name is Pratchett." ☐ 5 points

You've read *The Lord of the Rings* more than once. ☐ 1 point

You've read *The Lord of the Rings* more than ten times. ☐ 3 points

You've had to buy another copy of *The Lord of the Rings* because you read your old one so much, the spine broke.

☐ 5 points

You've moved a *Doctor Who* novelization out of the children's section and into the science fiction section of a bookshop.

☐ 2 points

You've moved a *Doctor Who* novelization out of the science fiction section and into the literary classics section of a bookshop.

☐ 4 points

You've taken a photograph of your comic, CD or DVD collection.

☐ 3 points

...you didn't do it for insurance purposes.

☐ 5 points

You've found an Easter egg on a DVD or computer game.

☐ 1 point

You've gone to great lengths to remove a label from a book or DVD without damaging it, such as steaming it off.

☐ 3 points

YOU OWN A DYMO LABELING MACHINE.

☐ 1 POINT

YOU'VE USED IT TO CATEGORIZE YOUR DVD OR CD COLLECTION.

☐ 3 POINTS

You can never truly get into a game, band, movie, website, book or graphic novel unless you liked it before all your friends.

☐ 1 point

You've bought a record, book or comic as an investment.

☐ 2 points

You've written the release date of a CD, DVD or computer game in your calendar.

☐ 2 points

ARE YOU A GEEK?

You've made a list of all the books you want to read, DVDs you want to watch and games you want to complete, and calculated that you would have to live to 90 in order to do so. And that's based on the assumption that nothing good will ever be released again.

3 points

Total points for this section:

Total points so far:

• HOBBIES •

You've been to a pub quiz.

☐ 1 point

You've disputed an answer given by a pub quizmaster.

☐ 3 points

You've gone home to fetch a reference book to disprove an answer given by a pub quizmaster.

☐ 4 points

You've been banned from a pub quiz.

☐ 5 points

You're a Trekkie.

☐ 4 points

You refused to tick the above box because you prefer the term "Trekker."

☐ 5 points

You're a trainspotter.

☐ 4 points

You refused to tick the above box because you prefer the term "rail enthusiast."

☐ 5 points

You own a train set.

☐ 4 points

You refused to tick the above box because you refer to it as your "scale model railway."

☐ 5 points

You're a fan of comics.

☐ 4 points

You can fill in the following channel numbers:

The Sci-Fi Channel _____ ☐ **1 point**

The Playboy Channel _____ ☐ **2 points**

The Discovery Channel _____ ☐ **3 points**

The History Channel _____ ☐ **4 points**

The Science Channel _____ ☐ **5 points**

You refused to tick the previous box because you prefer the term "graphic novels." ☐ **5 points**

You're into sports. ☐ **–1 point**

...but only in the sense that you enjoy watching them on TV and memorizing statistics rather than actually playing them. ☐ **3 points**

You've been to a fan signing session. ☐ **1 point**

You've been to a fan convention. ☐ **3 points**

You've been on a fan cruise. ☐ **5 points**

You've watched a dreadful TV movie just because it had someone from your favorite sci-fi show in it. ☐ **4 points**

You've watched the shopping channel because it had someone from your favorite sci-fi show hosting it. ☐ **5 points**

When you were asked what activities you enjoy at your last job interview, you said that you like dressing up as a wizard and acting out fantasy battles in the woods.

☐ 3 points

You genuinely couldn't understand why you didn't get the job.

☐ 5 points

You automatically tried to click on this sentence, before remembering that you're reading a book.

☐ 2 points

You often look up the price of your vintage toy collection on eBay, even though you wouldn't sell it even if it meant you had to starve.

☐ 2 points

You were charged with wasting police time when you phoned them up at 3 A.M. to tell them that you'd just cracked four murders from your *Unsolved Murder Casebook*.

☐ 5 points

• BONUS POINTS •

You were a member of the following clubs at college:

Juggling

☐ 1 point

Coin collecting

☐ 2 points

Heraldry

☐ 3 points

Astronomy

☐ 4 points

Science Fiction

☐ 5 points

ARE YOU A GEEK?

You've been go-carting, paintballing or laser-tagging with a group of friends.

☐ 1 point

You've been go-carting, paintballing or laser-tagging on your own, so you could beat your friends the next time you went with them.

☐ 3 points

You've been to a planetarium.

☐ 1 point

You've invented your own rules for a board game such as Monopoly, Clue or Risk.

☐ 2 points

You've bought a themed chess set.

☐ 3 points

You've bought a themed edition of Monopoly, Clue or Risk.

☐ 3 points

You've sung the *Jeopardy!* theme to make someone hurry up while playing a board game.

☐ 3 points

You've been to a specialty shop for magicians.

☐ 3 points

You have a collection of interesting-looking rocks that you've picked up while walking in the countryside.

☐ 1 point

Your local paper has run a story about you and one of your collections.

☐ 3 points

You were proud of the story and sent a copy to everyone you knew.

☐ 5 points

You've attempted to travel the entire subway network in a day.

☐ 5 points

You've cut a grape in half and put it in your microwave to try to create a glowing ball of plasma.

☐ 3 points

Select "History" from the menu of your Internet browser and write down the names of the last ten websites you've visited:

1 ....
2 ....
3 ....
4 ....
5 ....
6 ....
7 ....
8 ....
9 ....
10 ....

Award yourself a point for every porn site you visited. ◯ **points**

Award yourself three points for every bulletin board about sci-fi, conspiracy theories or astronomy you visited. ◯ **points**

Award yourself five points for every online role-playing game site you visited. ◯ **points**

You've got your own website. ☐ **1 point**

...and it contains your blog. ☐ **2 points**

...and it contains pictures of you with your various collections. ☐ **3 points**

...and you've included a series of FAQs about yourself. ☐ **4 points**

ARE YOU A GEEK?

...and less than five people have ever signed your guest book.

☐ 5 points

You've searched for people with the same name as you using Google.

☐ 1 point

You've printed out pictures of people with the same name as you that you found using Google.

☐ 3 points

You've emailed people with the same name as you that you've found using Google.

☐ 5 points

You own a metal detector.

☐ 2 points

While you were buying a toy for yourself, a shop assistant has asked you the name of the child you were buying it for.

☐ 2 points

You can't understand why your friend Graham has lost his enthusiasm for role-playing games since he lost his virginity.

☐ 5 points

•BONUS POINTS•

You collect...

stamps

☐ 1 point

manga

☐ 2 points

pogs

☐ 3 points

PEZ dispensers

☐ 4 points

war memorabilia

☐ 5 points

HOBBIES

You've bought a replica of a fantasy sword. 3 points

You've kept everyone at work waiting to use the printer while you printed out the 100-page walk-through for the game you were stuck on. 3 points

You've kept everyone at work waiting to use the printer while you printed out the 100-page sci-fi movie script you were working on. 5 points

You've bought some paint in the color "Orc Green." 3 points

You've sent yourself a letter in order to patent an idea for an invention that you've had. 5 points

You've bought a puzzle magazine. 2 points

You've drawn pictures of what you think extraterrestrials would look like. 3 points

...which included detailed diagrams of their genitals. 5 points

If you've read a Fighting Fantasy Gamebook, turn to page 1000101 (69). If you haven't, keep reading.

You've spent a weekend re-creating a famous historical battle. 3 points

You've been to a monster truck show. 3 points

You've been to a live WWE show. 3 points

You own some original comic art. 4 points

You own an animation cel. 5 points

ARE YOU A GEEK?

You've bought a display folder to protect your trading cards. ☐ **2 points**

You've kept a scrapbook about one of your hobbies. ☐ **2 points**

You've kept a scrapbook about someone you were obsessed with. ☐ **4 points**

You've sent a fan letter to your favorite celebrity. ☐ **1 point**

You've sent some fan fiction to your favorite celebrity. ☐ **2 points**

You've waited outside the house of your favorite celebrity so you could deliver the fan fiction personally. ☐ **3 points**

...and couldn't resist a quick look through their trash cans while you were waiting. ☐ **4 points**

You're not allowed within 50 feet of your favorite celebrity. ☐ **5 points**

You own life-size cardboard cutouts of sci-fi characters. ☐ **3 points**

You've partied with your life-size cardboard cutouts of sci-fi characters. ☐ **5 points**

To you, "charisma" is a characteristic of role-playing games characters. ☐ **2 points**

You've read the following:

A graphic novel by Neil Gaiman	1 point		A book by Stephen King	1 point
A graphic novel by Alan Moore	1 point		A book of unfinished fragments of Tolkien's writings	1 point
A book with the words "the science of" in the title	1 point		A technical manual about a science fiction show	1 point
A book with the words "the art of" in the title	1 point		A book about the paranormal	1 point
A book with the words "the companion to" in the title	1 point		A book of hints and solutions for a computer game	1 point
A book by Isaac Asimov	1 point		A popular science book	1 point
A book by Piers Anthony	1 point		A trilogy	1 point
A book by Arthur C. Clarke	1 point		A quadrilogy	1 point
A book by Robert Jordan	1 point		A cycle	1 point
A book by Douglas Adams	1 point			
A book by Anne McCaffrey	1 point		**Total**	points

You've bought some cardboard-backed plastic bags especially designed to stop your comics from deteriorating from mint condition to near-mint condition.

2 points

You've spent so long using your mouse that your wrist hurts.

1 point

You have a spreadsheet program on your home computer.

1 point

ARE YOU A GEEK?

You've actually used it for something that didn't relate to work, like logging your CD or DVD collection.

☐ 3 points

The main emotion you feel when you see a newborn baby is jealousy, because they'll probably live to see much more new technology than you.

☐ 2 points

The Tamagotchi you bought in 1996 is still alive and well, and you feed it every day.

☐ 2 points

YOU CAN WRITE IN RUNES.

☐ 1 point

You can write calligraphy.

☐ 1 point

As a teenager, you had the complete set of *How to Play Electric Guitar* books, and you can still play any public domain tune as if it were a heavy-metal guitar solo.

☐ 2 points

You've bought Japanese comics, toys or DVDs over the Internet.

☐ 3 points

You've bought Japanese girls' knickers over the Internet.

☐ 5 points

The hairs on the back of your neck still stand up when you hear the phrase "Prepare for battle . . . in *Robot Wars*."

☐ 2 points

You've approached a TV star in the street.

☐ 1 point

...and referred to them by the name of their fictional character.

☐ 3 points

...and presented them with a list of factual inaccuracies you've spotted in their TV show.

☐ 5 points

Now that you've got a job, you spend all your money buying the things you wanted when you were a child, like Optimus Prime or Castle Greyskull.

☐ 3 points

HOBBIES

You don't understand why people think your collection of *Spider-Man* comics is geeky. After all, it's the *Wolverine* fans that are geeky.

☐ **5 points**

You've filled in a character sheet.

☐ **5 points**

Geek Character Sheet

Name: _____

Alignment: Good/Evil

Weapons: _____

Languages: _____

_____

_____

Magic items

Ring of invisibility ☐

Cloak of displacement ☐

Force-field robe ☐

Long-distance crossbow ☐

iPod ☐

Ability

STR ____

DEX ____

CON ____

INT ____

WIS ____

CHR ____

Character Sketch

[ ]

Skills

Spellcraft ☐

Alchemy ☐

Knowledge (Arcana) ☐

Knowledge (Math) ☐

Knowledge (Film) ☐

If you have a die with more than six sides in your house, roll it and award yourself that many points.

◯ **points**

You've referred to a price guide in the last month.

☐ **5 points**

Total points for this section:

Total points so far:

ARE YOU A GEEK?

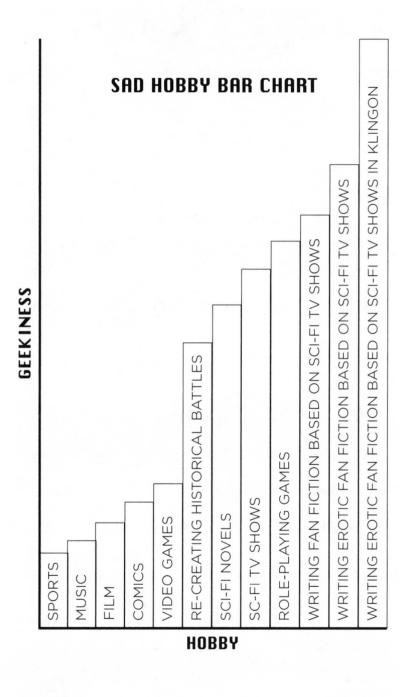

SAD HOBBY BAR CHART

GEEKINESS

HOBBY

SPORTS

MUSIC

FILM

COMICS

VIDEO GAMES

RE-CREATING HISTORICAL BATTLES

SCI-FI NOVELS

SC-FI TV SHOWS

ROLE-PLAYING GAMES

WRITING FAN FICTION BASED ON SCI-FI TV SHOWS

WRITING EROTIC FAN FICTION BASED ON SCI-FI TV SHOWS

WRITING EROTIC FAN FICTION BASED ON SCI-FI TV SHOWS IN KLINGON

The Male Geek's Version

You've had sex. ☐ −3 points

...but you did it to a Led Zeppelin album. ☐ 3 points

...but you did it to a They Might Be Giants album. ☐ 5 points

You have a girlfriend. ☐ −3 points

...but you met her through an online dating agency. ☐ 3 points

...but you met her at a Neil Gaiman signing. ☐ 5 points

You're married. ☐ −3 points

...but you met your wife in a web chat room. ☐ 3 points

...but you met your wife by clicking on a banner ad for Russian brides. ☐ 5 points

You've created a fake nude image of Sarah Michelle Gellar using Photoshop. ☐ 2 points

You had a crush on the only girl in your physics class at college. ☐ 2 points

You had a recurring sexual fantasy in which she was an elfin queen and you were a mighty warrior.

☐ 4 points

You've thrown away condoms because they were past their expiration date.

☐ 4 points

You've watched a female wrestling match.

☐ 2 points

You've watched adult manga.

☐ 3 points

You've told someone that your baldness is a sign of high testosterone.

☐ 1 point

...as a pick-up line.

☐ 3 points

To you, "Trojan" means an innocent-looking program that actually damages your computer, rather than a brand of condoms.

☐ 1 point

You've just turned to this page from page 111110 (62).

☐ 5 points

You're waiting until you get to that age when women learn to see past physical appearances and start to look for men with personality instead.

☐ 1 point

• BONUS POINTS •

The only man you would compromise your heterosexuality for is...

Keanu Reeves

☐ 1 point

Mark Hamill

☐ 2 points

Leonard Nimoy, especially if he sang "The Ballad of Bilbo Baggins" to you throughout

☐ 5 points

You're waiting until you get to that age when women learn to see past personality and start to look for any single male instead.

☐ 3 points

You've had a sexual fantasy about Gillian Anderson.

☐ 1 point

You've had sexual fantasies about all of the female *Doctor Who* companions.

☐ 3 points

...including Bonnie Langford.

☐ 5 points

You've found yourself sexually attracted to a video game character.

☐ 2 points

You were still a virgin on your 21st birthday.

☐ 1 point

You were still a virgin on your 30th birthday.

☐ 3 points

You are in your late thirties and still a virgin.

☐ 5 points

When seducing someone, you mention interesting sex facts, such as that male iguanas have two penises, the male octopus has its genitals on its head and the female praying mantis initiates sex by ripping the male's head off.

☐ 4 points

You walked out of the last date you were on when you asked your date what her favorite albums were, and she listed greatest hits compilations rather than actual albums.

☐ 2 points

You've been too scared to talk to a girl you liked, so you scratched her name on your arm with a knife and showed it to her instead.

☐ 3 points

You've used the "zoom" function on your DVD player.

☐ 4 points

ARE YOU A GEEK?

You've fantasized about the sexiest girl in your office wearing Princess Leia's *Return of the Jedi* costume.

☐ 1 point

You're one of over 30 guys who have a crush on the girl who works in the comic shop and actually knows quite a lot about manga.

☐ 1 point

Your sex life was transformed when you got broadband.

☐ 1 point

You've masturbated in the last week.

☐ 1 point

You've masturbated today.

☐ 2 points

You've masturbated in the last hour.

☐ 3 points

It was when you read the words "Gillian" and "Anderson" in this book.

☐ 5 points

You've wasted an hour of your life trying to decide which of two movie actresses you'd sleep with if you had the choice.

☐ 3 points

You've placed a personal ad.

☐ 1 point

It listed your strengths as "good knowledge of important historical battles and good understanding of how most machines work."

☐ 5 points

Total points for this section:

Total points so far:

The Female Geek's Version

You've had sex. □ –3 points

...but you were dressed as an elfin queen at the time. □ 3 points

...but you were dressed as Princess Leia in *Return of the Jedi* at the time. □ 5 points

You have a boyfriend. □ –3 points

•BONUS POINTS•

To you, "fingering" means...

manual vaginal stimulation □ –5 points

looking up someone's email address on the Internet □ 5 points

To you, "scoring" means...

hooking up with a member of the opposite sex □ –5 points

using a d20 to attribute abilities to the Dungeons and Dragons character you are creating □ 5 points

To you, the acronym DVDA stands for...

Digital Versatile Disc Audio □ 4 points

Double Vaginal, Double Anal (the holy grail of porn shots) □ 5 points

ARE YOU A GEEK?

...but he calls you "Arwen" and you call him "Aragorn."

☐ 3 points

...but he's a cyber boyfriend.

☐ 5 points

You're married.

☐ –3 points

...but you met your husband at a fan convention.

☐ 3 points

...but you got married in a Star Fleet uniform.

☐ 5 points

You've read a piece of erotic fan fiction.

☐ 2 points

You've written a piece of erotic fan fiction.

☐ 3 points

You've written a piece of erotic fan fiction featuring yourself.

☐ 4 points

You've written a piece of erotic fan fiction featuring yourself and a sci-fi actor and sent it to him via his agent.

☐ 5 points

When you got your first boyfriend at college, you made a big point of PDA, to make up for all the sexual rejection you'd encountered previously in life.

☐ 1 point

You've had a sexual fantasy about Data.

☐ 1 point

You've had a sexual fantasy about Gimli.

☐ 3 points

You've had a sexual fantasy about Terry Pratchett.

☐ 5 points

You've deliberately gotten into a dull, male-dominated hobby just to increase your chances of hooking up.

☐ 1 point

You've blown off a guy in a bar because you were looking forward to going home and playing Zelda.

☐ 1 point

You feel oddly attracted to the following nonhumans:

Data

☐ 1 point

Chewbacca

☐ 3 points

Alf

☐ 5 points

You've told someone that Valentine's Day is a shallow marketing exercise invented by greeting card companies.

☐ 3 points

You did this to change the subject when someone asked you how many Valentine cards you'd received.

☐ 5 points

You've pretended to someone that you had a boyfriend.

☐ 1 point

You didn't do this to avoid unwanted attention in a nightclub.

☐ 3 points

You're attracted to men with long, greasy hair.

☐ 3 points

You've been too scared to talk to a guy you liked, so you wrote a poem about him instead.

☐ 1 point

It was written in a precise form, such as a sonnet or a haiku.

☐ 3 points

You've exchanged mobile numbers with a guy you met in a nightclub.

☐ –1 point

You phoned him five times in the next 24 hours, and he told you never to call him again.

☐ 3 points

ARE YOU A GEEK?

You're usually the one who makes the first move. ☐ 1 point

You're usually the one who gets dumped. ☐ 3 points

You've been the only singleton at a dinner party. ☐ 1 point

You've never taken a shower with a guy you've just hooked up with. ☐ 2 points

You've never taken a shower. ☐ 5 points

You've used a dating agency. ☐ 3 points

You own a vibrator. ☐ 1 point

You've used it in the last week. ☐ 2 points

You've used it today. ☐ 3 points

It was when you read the word "Data" in this book. ☐ 5 points

Geekline

☐ Please send me my compatibility test in total confidence.

My gender is: Male ☐ Female ☐

My age is ....
My height is ....
First name ....
Surname ....
Elvish name ....
Address ....
....
Email address 1 ....
Email address 2 ....
Email address 3 ....
Email address 4 ....
Email address 5 ....

Tick the boxes that best describe you:
☐ Shy   ☐ Overweight
☐ Introverted   ☐ Unkempt
☐ Obsessive   ☐ Anally retentive
☐ Sarcastic   ☐ Stalker
☐ Pedantic   ☐ Bunny boiler

Tick the activities that you enjoy:
☐ Stamp collecting
☐ Coin collecting
☐ Memorizing phone books
☐ Dressing up as Middle Earth characters
☐ Just sitting and staring at the wall
☐ ST: TOS
☐ ST: TNG
☐ ST: DS9
☐ ST: VOY
☐ ST: ENT

You've gone to a bookshop specifically to try and hook up.

☐ 3 points

You've replied to a personal ad.

☐ 1 point

In it, the guy listed his strengths as "good knowledge of historical battles and understanding of how most machines work."

☐ 5 points

Total points for this section:

Total points so far:

ARE YOU A GEEK?

You can multiply large numbers together without using a calculator.

☐ 1 point

...or a piece of paper.

☐ 3 points

When someone tells you what their date of birth is, you can instantly tell them what day of the week it fell on.

☐ 3 points

When someone drops some toothpicks on the floor, you can instantly tell them how many they've dropped.

☐ 5 points

You've drawn a map from memory.

☐ 4 points

...it was the fantasy landscape of a book.

☐ 5 points

You can count in binary.

☐ 0011 points

You can count in hexadecimal.

☐ A points

You understand the following jokes:

A neutron walks into a bar, orders a beer and begins to open his wallet when the barman says, "For you, no charge."

☐ 1 point

There are only 10 types of people in this world—those who understand binary and those who don't.

☐ 3 points

Why do programmers mix up Halloween and Christmas? Because OCT 31 = DEC 25.

☐ 5 points

You've overanalyzed a joke. So, for example, when someone has asked you, "What's the difference between a sorority girl and the *Titanic*?" you've told them that the two things have more than one difference, so it's difficult to isolate a single one.

☐ 5 points

ARE YOU A GEEK?

Fill in your exam results below.

Year	Subject	Grade
....	....	....
....	....	....
....	....	....
....	....	....
....	....	....
....	....	....
....	....	....
....	....	....
....	....	....
....	....	....
....	....	....
....	....	....
....	....	....
....	....	....
....	....	....
....	....	....
....	....	....

Please continue on a separate sheet if necessary

Add your high school grade point average to your score. ◯ points

Divide your math SAT score by 100 and add it to your score. ◯ points

You were the valedictorian of your high school class. ☐ 3 points

You got an A in Math, Physics, Biology or Chemistry. ☐ 3 points

...and you still look over your notes for fun. ☐ 4 points

You competed in a math league. ☐ 4 points

...and referred to yourself as a "mathlete." ☐ 5 points

You have a Ph.D. ☐ 4 points

...it's in math, astrophysics or folklore mythology. ☐ 5 points

---

•BONUS POINTS•

You've realized that the following are anagrams:

The Morse Code = Here come dots ☐ 1 point

Snooze alarms = Alas! No more Zs ☐ 2 points

A decimal point = I'm a dot in place ☐ 3 points

Eleven plus two = Twelve plus one ☐ 4 points

Soylent Green = Stolen energy ☐ 5 points

ARE YOU A GEEK?

You've tried to use the following palindromes in everyday conversation:

Don't nod ☐ 1 point

Lager, sir, is regal ☐ 2 points

Rise to vote, sir ☐ 3 points

Rats live on no evil star ☐ 4 points

Are we not drawn onward, we few? Drawn onward to new era? ☐ 5 points

---

You've corrected a fact in a lecture. ☐ 1 point

You've laughed at a joke made in a lecture. ☐ 2 points

You've laughed at a joke you didn't find funny, just to prove that you understood it. ☐ 3 points

You get more pleasure from making a joke that goes over people's heads than one that makes them laugh. ☐ 4 points

You're a member of Mensa. ☐ 3 points

You spent the last Mensa party talking at length about what a ridiculous misconception it is that intellectually superior people don't know how to party. ☐ 5 points

You've conducted a scientific experiment for your own pleasure. ☐ 3 points

INTELLIGENCE

You've listed the premises of an argument you were disputing.

☐ 3 points

You've written out a logical formula to prove that your argument was right.

☐ 5 points

You can recite ten or more Monty Python sketches in their entirety.

☐ 2 points

...but you can't remember the names of most people in your office.

☐ 3 points

...or which is left and which is right.

☐ 5 points

•BONUS POINTS•

You know the answers to these famous lateral-thinking puzzles:

A man walks into a bar and asks for a glass of water. The barman takes out a gun and points it at him. The man says "Thank you" and leaves. Why?

☐ 1 point

A man is pushing his car. When he gets to a hotel, he knows he's bankrupt. Why?

☐ 1 point

A woman is walking down the stairs when the lights go out. She knows her husband is dead. How?

☐ 1 point

A dead man hangs from a rafter in the middle of an empty room. The nearest wall is over ten feet away. How did he kill himself?

☐ 1 point

A man is going toward a field. He's carrying a pack on his back. He knows that when he gets to the field he will die. Why?

☐ 1 point

ARE YOU A GEEK?

You'd feel proud of yourself if you broke the following world records:

The most times that the Lord's Prayer has been written on the back of a postage stamp ☐ **1 point**

The longest time spent continually going up and down escalators ☐ **2 points**

Typing the numbers one to a million in words in the fastest time ☐ **3 points**

The longest time spent standing motionless ☐ **4 points**

Discovering the largest known prime number ☐ **5 points**

You can't imagine what it must be like never to have wondered what the function keys are for. ☐ **1 point**

You've had a conversation about the paradoxes of time travel. ☐ **2 points**

You've devised an anagram of your name. ☐ **1 point**

...and of the names of everyone in your office. ☐ **2 points**

...and sent them out on a public email. ☐ **3 points**

You've devised a palindrome that included your name. ☐ **4 points**

You've devised a riddle. ☐ **5 points**

You find the following acts of multitasking difficult:

Driving and changing the radio station at the same time
☐ 1 point

Watching TV and reading a magazine at the same time
☐ 3 points

Walking and talking at the same time
☐ 5 points

You've explained in great detail why an urban legend must be false. So, for example, if someone's told you that Chinese restaurants kill cats and dogs for meat, you've explained to them why doing this would be less cost-effective than buying meat from a wholesaler.
☐ 2 points

You've completed a Sudoku puzzle with an "expert" difficulty level.
☐ 3 points

Spent a day talking like Yoda, you have.
☐ 4 points

Forfeit for losing at Trivial Pursuit, it was.
☐ −2 points

You find it hard to have a conversation with someone who doesn't have a Ph.D.
☐ 3 points

You've gotten annoyed at someone repeating a clearly untrue statistic, like that you're never more than 20 feet away from a rat.
☐ 1 point

You've gone into a detailed mathematical explanation about why their statistic is invalid.
☐ 3 points

ARE YOU A GEEK?

You've found a Googlewhack.

☐ 3 points

If there was a copy of *Scientific American* and *People* in your dentist's waiting room, you'd pick up the copy of *Scientific American*.

☐ 1 point

...or get your own copy of *Edge, Wired* or *The Journal of Computer Science & Technology* out of your bag.

☐ 3 points

You've criticized someone for using an inaccurate expression, as in "I could care less" when they mean "I *couldn't* care less."

☐ 1 point

You've used a protractor since leaving school.

☐ 1 point

You've completed a cryptic crossword.

☐ 1 point

...in under three minutes.

☐ 3 points

You've overheard some people trying to solve a crossword on a train, and couldn't resist shouting the answers at them.

☐ 5 points

You've told someone that your superior intellect is probably the reason you don't have many friends.

☐ 5 points

You've discussed the "emotional core," "subtext" or "denouement" of an episode of a sci-fi show.

☐ 3 points

You've spent more than an hour speculating on whether teleportation will ever be a scientific reality.

☐ 3 points

If someone at a bus stop complains to you that you wait ages for a bus and then three come along at once, you go into a detailed explanation about why this always happens.

☐ 5 points

INTELLIGENCE

You've spent so long reading that you find it difficult to interact with the physical world, and have trouble making coffee or pouring milk onto a bowl of cereal.

☐ 1 point

You've memorized a list of prime numbers.

☐ 2 points

You've wondered if your PIN is a prime number.

☐ 3 points

...and worked it out.

☐ 4 points

...without using a calculator.

☐ 5 points

You know what your IQ is
(award yourself your IQ in points).

◯ points

Total points for this section:

Total points so far:

ARE YOU A GEEK?

You've interrupted a conversation to point out a factual inaccuracy.

☐ 1 point

You've interrupted a pub conversation to tell everyone that you've identified what the obscure song playing on the jukebox is.

☐ 1 point

You also told them the song's highest chart position, and the number of weeks it spent on the chart.

☐ 3 points

You've interrupted a conversation to identify the species of a nearby bird.

☐ 3 points

You've won an argument by quoting a statistic that you've memorized.

☐ 1 point

You've shouted at the TV when a contestant has gotten an easy answer wrong on a quiz show.

☐ 1 point

You've jotted down interesting facts in a notebook while watching the Discovery Channel.

☐ 3 points

You've told someone a historical fact relating to a nearby landmark.

☐ 3 points

While on a tour of a site of historical interest, you've corrected a fact that the guide has told the group.

☐ 3 points

You can fill in the blank periodic table below.

5 points

ARE YOU A GEEK?

You've read the entire instruction manual before using a new piece of technology.

☐ 1 point

You find that you enjoy using gadgets much more when you understand exactly how they work.

☐ 3 points

If someone is having trouble with visual aids in a meeting at work, you automatically go up to fix them, without waiting to be asked.

☐ 3 points

You've recited a series of facts about the health risks of smoking when asking someone to put a cigarette out.

☐ 1 point

You've given someone a long and detailed description about the quickest way to get between two places by car or public transportation.

☐ 1 point

You've recited a dictionary definition to someone who was using a word incorrectly.

☐ 3 points

•BONUS POINTS•

You've corrected people on the following misquotations:

That Captain Kirk said, "Beam me up, Scotty."

☐ 1 point

That Sherlock Holmes said, "Elementary, my dear Watson."

☐ 1 point

That Humphrey Bogart said, "Play it again, Sam" in Casablanca.

☐ 1 point

That Tarzan said, "Me Tarzan, you Jane."

☐ 1 point

That James Cagney said, "You dirty rat!"

☐ 1 point

You've appeared on the following quiz or game shows:

Jeopardy! ☐ 5 points

Beat the Geeks ☐ 5 points

Who Wants to Be a Millionaire? ☐ 5 points

Remote Control ☐ 5 points

Win Ben Stein's Money ☐ 5 points

Wheel of Fortune ☐ −5 points

You've listed multiple dictionary definitions of a word that someone has just used, and asked them to clarify which one they meant. ☐ 2 points

You've corrected someone's pronunciation of a word. ☐ 2 points

You've interrupted someone to correct they're grammar. ☐ 3 points

You noticed the grammatical mistake in the above sentence, and you were just about to email in and complain. ☐ 5 points

You've interrupted someone to tell them the origin of the phrase they just used. ☐ 1 point

You get annoyed by split infinitives. ☐ 1 point

Except "To boldly go where no man has gone before." That one's allowed. ☐ 1 point

ARE YOU A GEEK?

You get annoyed by double negatives. ☐ **1 point**

Except "I ain't afraid of no ghost." That one's allowed. ☐ **1 point**

You get annoyed by everyday oxymorons like
"same difference," "plastic glass," "found missing,"
"virtually spotless" and "almost exactly." ☐ **1 point**

But you don't mind "living dead." That one's allowed. ☐ **1 point**

You get annoyed by everyday tautologies like "rough
approximation," "free gift," "new innovation" and
"significant milestone." ☐ **1 point**

You can fill in the values below.

Inches	0	1	2	3	4
Centimeters					

Miles	30	40	50	60	70	80
Kilometers						

Fahrenheit	0°	32°		212°
Centigrade				

☐ **5 points**

You've corrected the grammar of a piece of graffiti. ☐ **2 points**

You've boycotted a "five items or less"
supermarket line on the grounds that "fewer"
and not "less" is the correct word to use when
describing countable nouns. ☐ **2 points**

You've pointed out that the correct plural form of
"matrix" is "matrices." ☐ **2 points**

You've pointed out that the correct singular
form of "data" is "datum." ☐ **2 points**

You've pointed out that the correct singular form of "dice" is "die."

☐ 3 points

You did this while using a die with 20 sides.

☐ 4 points

...which you referred to as a "d20."

☐ 5 points

You can tell which word is mispelled—"conscientious," "recommend," "separate," "embarrass," "obsolescent," "parallel," "tendency," "mischievous," "surreptitious," "roommate," "ironically," "drunkenness," "guarantee," "pastime," "necessary."

☐ 1 point

You know your Hobbit and Elvish name.

☐ 3 points

You've used the word "whom" in its correct context. ☐ 1 point

---

•BONUS POINTS•

You've noticed, and complained about, these redundant acronyms:

PIN number (Personal Identification Number number)

☐ 1 point

ATM machine (Automatic Teller Machine machine) ☐ 1 point

ISBN number (International Standard Book Number number)

☐ 1 point

LCD display (Liquid Crystal Display display)

☐ 1 point

HIV virus (Human Immunodeficiency Virus virus)

☐ 1 point

ARE YOU A GEEK?

You can speak the following languages:

Japanese ☐ 1 point

Esperanto ☐ 2 points

Elvish ☐ 3 points

Klingon ☐ 4 points

C++ ☐ 5 points

You've used the following words when playing
Scrabble: "qi," "zo," "jo," "xu," "xi," "ax," "yu," "ny," "ka," "ko." ☐ 1 point

You've dipped into a dictionary for pleasure. ☐ 1 point

You've read a dictionary cover to cover for pleasure. ☐ 3 points

It was an Elvish or Klingon dictionary. ☐ 5 points

You saw that, although this paragraph looks ordinary, it is
actually unusual. That a particular common symbol is
missing. And that this particular handicap allows only
consonants and A, I, O and U. That is to say, you saw
that this is a lipogram. ☐ 1 point

You know what a TLA is. ☐ 1 point

...and that there are 26^3 possible ones in existence. ☐ 3 points

You've filled an uncomfortable silence in the pub by
explaining to everyone that glass is actually a liquid. ☐ 2 points

KNOWLEDGE

While discussing martial arts movies, you've told someone that Bruce Lee was so fast that the filmmakers had to slow down the footage, rather than speed it up like they normally do.

☐ 1 point

You can link Kevin Bacon to any other movie star in six moves.

☐ 2 points

You've pointed out to someone that "Big Ben" is the name of the largest bell, not the clock itself.

☐ 1 point

If someone tells you that black is their favorite color, you point out that it's not actually a color, but the absence of all colors.

☐ 1 point

• BONUS POINTS •

You've given the following pedantic responses:

Them: Are you looking for a punch in the face or something?

You: I am looking for something, but that something is not a punch in the face.

☐ 1 point

Them: Just shut up and tell me what you think.

You: How can I shut up and tell you what I think?

☐ 1 point

Them: Can I ask you to hold this for me?

You: Yes, you can ask me to hold that for you.

☐ 1 point

Them: Is someone sitting there?

You: No, someone is not sitting there, but somebody will be sitting there when they return from the bathroom.

☐ 1 point

Them: Are you still here?

You: Given that you can see me and we're having a conversation, I think it's safe to assume that I'm still here.

☐ 1 point

ARE YOU A GEEK?

As soon as your watch displays 12:00:00, you start saying "Good afternoon" to people instead of "Good morning."

☐ 3 points

When someone calls you anally retentive, you point out that the term refers to someone who's retained the anal stage of Freudian psychosexual development, rather than someone who's just obsessed with detail.

☐ 1 point

However, rather than accepting their mistake, they tend to cite this as further proof that you're anally retentive.

☐ 3 points

You know how to interpret Tarot cards.

☐ 1 point

...and you've referred to yourself as a "mystic" while doing so.

☐ 3 points

While making the point that bottled water is a waste of money, you've pointed out that "Evian" spelled backward is "naïve."

☐ 1 point

You've corrected a common misconception, such as that millipedes have a thousand legs.

☐ 3 points

You've corrected someone on the misconception that the Great Wall of China is the only man-made object that's visible from space, and pointed out that, as "space" starts at roughly 60 miles above the surface of the earth, thousands of man-made objects can be seen from it, including electric lights.

☐ 5 points

You can read Roman numerals.

☐ III points

Ÿou ĸnoш ŧhe ŧhree laшs of robotics.

☐ ∃ points

Ÿou ĸnoш ŧhe zeroŧh laш of robotics.

☐ ꟼ points

You konw taht the huamn mnid deos not raed ervey lteter in a wrod, but the wrod as a wlohe, so as lnog as the frist and last ltteers are in the rghit pclae, you will be albe to uesdnatnrd it.

☐ 1 pnoit

KNOWLEDGE   1011111 [**95**]

You can recognize over 100 fonts.

☐ 1 point

Including this one.

☐ 3 points

And you hate this one.

☐ 3 points

You boycotted all parties on New Year's Eve 1999 on the grounds that technically the third millennium did not start until the end of the year 2000.

☐ 1 point

You wanted to boycott all parties on New Year's Eve 1999, but you weren't invited to any.

☐ 2 points

You've corrected someone who thought that "legos" was the plural of "lego."

☐ 1 point

You've pointed out to someone that an April Fools' joke doesn't count if it's done after 12 P.M.

☐ 1 point

However, this didn't stop the person in question from laughing at the fact that you'd just fallen off the chair they'd taken the screws out of.

☐ 3 points

You know what "jumping the shark" is.

☐ 1 point

And you know exactly when *Red Dwarf, Star Trek* and *The X-Files* did it.

☐ 3 points

You've told someone that *Doctor Who* is the name of the program, not the main character, who's called "The Doctor."

☐ 3 points

You've told someone what TARDIS is an acronym for.

☐ 1 point

It ruins your entire day if you forget what a certain acronym stands for.

☐ 1 point

ARE YOU A GEEK?

ISBN 0-0919-0612-1

9 780091 906122

You can read bar codes.

☐ 1 point

You believe that every bar code features the number 666, and that this is a sign of the impending global apocalypse.

☐ 3 points

You've told someone where the name "Hotmail" derives from.

☐ 1 point

You've pointed out to someone that "Frankenstein" is the name of the creator, not the monster.

☐ 1 point

You've told someone that a certain invention was predicted years in advance by science fiction. So, for example, you've told them that *The Hitchhiker's Guide to the Galaxy* effectively predicted mobile Internet access.

☐ 1 point

You've executed a practical joke that used scientific knowledge, like putting methylene blue in someone's drink to make their urine blue.

☐ 3 points

When the film *Krakatoa, East of Java* comes on TV, you point out to everyone that Krakatoa is actually west of Java.

☐ 2 points

You've pointed out an inaccurate or unlikely use of technology in a film, as when the aliens' computers in *Independence Day* turn out to be Mac-compatible.

☐ 1 point

After watching a film with a race in it, you've given someone a detailed explanation of how the race could have been completed quicker.

☐ 1 point

When watching a film on TV with someone else, you refuse to answer questions about the plot, like "Is he a goodie or a baddie?" and "Is that the same guy we saw earlier?"

☐ 1 point

KNOWLEDGE

You've quoted a line from a sci-fi film in normal conversation.

☐ 1 point

...but nobody you were talking to picked up on the reference.

☐ 3 points

ARE YOU A GEEK?

You've pointed out that the following are urban legends:

Pigeons explode when they eat uncooked rice. ☐ **1 point**

Charles Manson auditioned for The Monkees. ☐ **1 point**

Walt Disney was cryogenically frozen. ☐ **1 point**

...and you were at a sci-fi convention. ☐ **5 points**

When you're watching an episode of *The Simpsons* with other people, you point out all the movie references in it. ☐ **1 point**

...except for the Kubrick, Hitchcock and Welles ones, which you regard as too obvious to point out. ☐ **3 points**

You've actually won money on those quiz machines in pubs. ☐ **5 points**

On the map opposite, color in all the countries that you know the capital cities of.

Award yourself three points if the map is more than half colored in. ☐ **3 points**

Award yourself five points if the map is fully colored in. ☐ **5 points**

Award yourself five points if you used a different colored pen for each continent. ☐ **5 points**

Award yourself five points if, while coloring the map in, you went over the lines and felt angry with yourself. ☐ **5 points**

KNOWLEDGE

You've been compared to the following fictional characters:

Beaker from The Muppet Show	1 point	*Brains from* Thunderbirds	1 point
Bert from Sesame Street	1 point	*Daria from* Daria and Beavis and Butthead	1 point
Comic Book Guy from The Simpsons	1 point	*Peter Parker before he becomes Spider-Man*	1 point
Millhouse from The Simpsons	1 point	*Max Fisher from* Rushmore	1 point
Professor Frink from The Simpsons	1 point	*Napoleon Dynamite*	1 point
Martin Prince from The Simpsons	1 point	*Brainy Smurf from* The Smurfs	1 point
Spock from Star Trek	1 point	*Velma from* Scooby-Doo	1 point
Data from Star Trek: The Next Generation	1 point	*Any character played by Anthony Michael Hall*	1 point
Wesley Crusher from Star Trek: The Next Generation	1 point	*Any character played by Jeff Goldblum*	1 point
Adric from Doctor Who	1 point		
Rimmer from Red Dwarf	1 point	**Total**	points

You know the Dewey Decimal System. ☐ 1 point

You've arranged all your books according to it. ☐ 3 points

Total points for this section:

Total points so far:

ARE YOU A GEEK?

You had braces.

☐ 1 point

You had acne.

☐ 1 point

You refused to believe in Santa because you didn't think it was possible that he could visit every house in the world in one night.

☐ 2 points

You refused to believe in Santa because you couldn't understand how operating a toy factory in the North Pole rather than, say, Taiwan was a viable economic option.

☐ 5 points

You had a Transformer.

☐ 1 point

...and it was Astrotrain, who transforms into a train.

☐ 3 points

You were deeply upset when one of your friends showed you a horror video, but only because the "pan and scan" did no justice to Dario Argento's original work.

☐ 5 points

Your parents tried to limit your computer or TV time to three hours a day to force you to play outside more.

☐ 1 point

You went to band camp.

☐ 1 point

You played a musical instrument to entertain friends of your parents.

☐ 1 point

You performed magic tricks to entertain friends of your parents.

☐ 3 points

You invented a secret language that only you and your friends knew the meaning of.

☐ 1 point

You invented a secret language that only you knew the meaning of.

☐ 3 points

You asked your parents for *Star Wars* figures for Christmas.

☐ 1 point

When you got them, you decided to leave them in their boxes so they'd be worth more in the future.

☐ 5 points

You asked your parents for a chemistry set for Christmas.

☐ 3 points

You still use it.

☐ 5 points

You would often get frustrated that games of Monopoly and Risk were over so soon, and that's how you got into Dungeons and Dragons.

☐ 3 points

The pop stars you most wanted to look like were Kraftwerk.

☐ 2 points

You had an imaginary friend.

☐ 1 point

You still talk to your imaginary friend occasionally.

☐ 3 points

You were the only student who didn't groan when the teacher announced a pop quiz.

☐ 2 points

ARE YOU A GEEK?

You attempted to win a schoolyard fight by using a Vulcan nerve pinch.

☐ 3 points

You won first prize in a science fair.

☐ 2 points

You were regarded as so dorky that your very name became a schoolyard insult. As in, "Stop being such a David."

☐ 4 points

You didn't get invited to the prom, so you decided to stay in and have a prom of your own . . . with your parents.

☐ 5 points

You actually laughed out loud when you had to watch a Shakespeare comedy in English class.

☐ 5 points

You had a subscription to *Microcomputing, Creative Computing, Byte, Run* or *Compute.*

☐ 1 point

Your fondest childhood memories all involve typing in BASIC programs that were transcribed in computer magazines.

☐ 5 points

You wrote your own computer games in BASIC.

☐ 2 points

•BONUS POINTS•

You tried to catch other kids out with the following trick questions:

If there are six apples and you take away four, how many do you have?

☐ 1 point

Which is heavier, a pound of feathers or a pound of gold?

☐ 1 point

How many bricks does it take to complete a building made entirely of bricks?

☐ 1 point

...and they contained no rude words whatsoever. That would have just been childish.

[ ] 4 points

The only sport you played was *Konami Track and Field.*

[ ] 1 point

When other children called you "sad," you said, "No, I'm not, I'm perfectly happy" as a comeback.

[ ] 1 point

When other children called you a bastard, you said, "Actually, I was born during wedlock."

[ ] 2 points

When other children called you a homo, you replied, "Yes, I am a *Homo sapiens,* if that's what you mean."

[ ] 3 points

When other children called you gay, you replied, "Yes, I am happy, lively, merry, playful and bright, if that is what you mean."

[ ] 4 points

...however, this didn't stop them running around the playground telling everyone that you just admitted you were gay.

[ ] 5 points

•BONUS POINTS•

You held one of the following positions at school:

School newspaper editor

[ ] 1 point

Captain of the debate team

[ ] 2 points

Captain of the spelling team

[ ] 3 points

Hall monitor

[ ] 4 points

Lab monitor

[ ] 5 points

ARE YOU A GEEK?

• BONUS POINTS •

You can remember the point of the following mnemonics:

Richard of York gave battle in vain ☐ 1 point

SOH-CAH-TOA ☐ 2 points

Kids prefer cheese over fried green spinach ☐ 3 points

Wow, I made a great discovery! ☐ 4 points

My very easy method: just set up nine planets ☐ 5 points

You were the first in your class to get a scientific calculator. ☐ 2 points

...and the last to get pubes. ☐ 4 points

The only time anyone tried to sit next to you in school was when there was a test. ☐ 1 point

You created a complex study timetable in the run-up to your exams. ☐ 1 point

You actually stuck to it. ☐ 2 points

You always sat in the front row in class. ☐ 2 points

You won the perfect attendance award. ☐ 1 point

You won the punctuality award. ☐ 3 points

You won the science award. ☐ 5 points

After watching the film *DARYL*, you devised an acronym to prove that you were also a robot, as in the following examples:

GRAHAM = General Robotic Artificial Humanoid Advanced Machine

KEITH = Kinetic Electronic Intelligent Technological Humanoid

KEN = Kinetic Electronic Neohuman

NIGEL = Networked Intelligent General Electronic Lifeform

BARRY = Biomechanical Analytic Robot: Replicant Youth

☐ 1 point

Award yourself a bonus point if your name actually is one of the ones used in the examples above.

☐ 1 point

You were slow-clapped when you went up to collect the award in assembly.

☐ 3 points

Everyone in your class tried your glasses on and did an impression of your voice.

☐ 3 points

You solved a Rubik's Cube in front of everyone else in assembly.

☐ 5 points

On your report card, you got an A for every subject except PE, in which you got an F.

☐ 1 point

When you used a long word in class, other pupils found it really funny, and shouted it at you for the rest of the day.

☐ 1 point

You tried to dissuade your friends from doing something that might lead to detention or suspension.

☐ 1 point

ARE YOU A GEEK?

You were the only pupil in your class who actually asked questions to visiting speakers.

☐ 3 points

You were the only pupil in your class who actually bought a lab coat when your science teacher recommended it.

☐ 3 points

You ran in the election at your school, with policies such as stronger punishments for litterbugs.

☐ 3 points

...and were beaten by a more popular child with a far less sophisticated manifesto.

☐ 5 points

You invented a mnemonic to help with your schoolwork.

☐ 3 points

In exams, you would annoy others by scribbling down pages of notes as soon as you saw the questions.

☐ 1 point

You would also finish your exam paper before the time had run out, and look smugly around at the kids who hadn't finished yet.

☐ 3 points

• BONUS POINTS •

You had the following trading card sets:

Star Wars, ET, Close Encounters of the Third Kind, or Raiders of the Lost Ark

☐ 1 point each

Garbage Pail Kids

☐ 2 points

Mars Attacks

☐ 3 points

Military Aircraft

☐ 4 points

U.S. Presidents

☐ 5 points

You brought packed lunches to school.

☐ 1 point

They included individually wrapped cheese slices, apples or cartons of fresh orange juice.

☐ 3 points

The science experiment that involved burning a magnesium strip wasn't the only one that you found interesting at school.

☐ 2 points

You had the horrible realization that other pupils were laughing at you rather than with you when you were reciting a passage from *The Hitchhiker's Guide to the Galaxy.*

☐ 5 points

The school bullies made you drink out of a lemonade bottle they'd all pissed in.

☐ 4 points

However, you had the last laugh, because you knew that human urine isn't toxic until it's passed through the body seven times.

☐ 5 points

•BONUS POINTS•

You were subject to the following forms of bullying at school:

Noogie

☐ 1 point

Wedgie

☐ 2 points

Glasses stamped on

☐ 3 points

RPG character sheet thrown into urinal

☐ 4 points

Head flushed down toilet

☐ 5 points

ARE YOU A GEEK?

You failed to do the following things in PE:

Complete the 1500 meters race

☐ **1 point**

Complete the 200 meters race

☐ **2 points**

Climb to the top of the rope in the gym

☐ **3 points**

A forward roll

☐ **4 points**

Throw overarm

☐ **5 points**

You couldn't understand why the school bullies didn't have more respect for someone who regularly got A's in science tests.

☐ **5 points**

When your class created a time capsule, you put a detailed project about modern living in it, rather than just a copy of *Tiger Beat, Teen Beat* or *Seventeen*.

☐ **2 points**

You dealt with aggression by writing angry poetry.

☐ **1 point**

The only days you ever played truant on were sports day and no uniform day.

☐ **1 point**

You were forced to compete in the egg-and-spoon race on sports day.

☐ **2 points**

You tried to reinvent yourself as one of the cool kids at school, before realizing it was too much effort and going back to the lunchtime role-playing games club.

☐ **1 point**

Your teacher relied on you to switch the TV onto the video channel.

☐ **1 point**

The teacher of another class relied on you to come into their class and switch the TV onto the video channel.

☐ 2 points

You refused to answer a question that a teacher asked you on the grounds that it was too easy.

☐ 3 points

When the teachers said you should spend an average of 90 minutes a night doing homework, you thought it sounded a bit low.

☐ 2 points

You asked a teacher for extra homework because you didn't think they'd given enough.

☐ 3 points

Another pupil is making rabbit ears behind your head with their fingers in your class photo.

☐ 3 points

You were home-schooled.

☐ 5 points

When you grew up, you wanted to be a train driver.

☐ 1 point

When you grew up, you wanted to be an astronaut.

☐ 3 points

When you grew up, you wanted to be a professor in mathematics at MIT.

☐ 5 points

At school, people used to throw your copy of *2000AD* around the class to make you chase after it.

☐ 3 points

At work, people throw your copy of *2000AD* around the office to make you chase after it.

☐ 5 points

You've posted a bitter message on classmates.com telling all the school bullies how much more than them you earn now.

☐ 5 points

Total points for this section:

ARE YOU A GEEK?

Total points so far:

You've owned any of the following toys or games (one point for each item you owned as a child, two points for each item you own now):

A Nintendo game and watch — 1 point / 2 points

A Styrofoam plane — 1 point / 2 points

A 3D Viewmaster — 1 point / 2 points

A radio-controlled car — 1 point / 2 points

A Rubik's Cube — 1 point / 2 points

Rubik's Revenge — 1 point / 2 points

A Slinky — 1 point / 2 points

The game Battleship — 1 point / 2 points

A Little Professor calculator — 1 point / 2 points

A He-Man figurine — 1 point / 2 points

A Star Wars figurine — 1 point / 2 points

A Dungeons and Dragons figurine — 1 point / 2 points

An airplane model kit — 1 point / 2 points

A jigsaw with over 5000 pieces — 1 point / 2 points

A 3D jigsaw — 1 point / 2 points

A magic kit — 1 point / 2 points

A telescope — 1 point / 2 points

A microscope — 1 point / 2 points

Magic Rocks, or any other crystal set — 1 point / 2 points

A Spirograph — 1 point / 2 points

Total ◯ points

You believe that *Star Wars* is the greatest film ever made.

☐ 1 point

You refused to check the above box because you refer to the first *Star Wars* movie as *A New Hope*.

☐ 2 points

You believe that when we die, we go to Valhalla.

☐ 2 points

You believe that when we die, we regenerate.

☐ 3 points

You believe that fractals are the most beautiful things in the world.

☐ 3 points

You believe that what we perceive as reality is merely an illusion created by mind-controlling machines.

☐ 3 points

You believe that Pitfall, Pole Position and Q-Bert were better than anything you can buy for the PlayStation 2.

☐ 3 points

You believe that your parallel-universe twin is a powerful magician researching into alchemy, rather than a biology student like yourself.

☐ 3 points

You believe that your parallel-universe twin is a king with many beautiful wives, and that one day you will cross over into that universe.

☐ 4 points

You believe that you have a birthmark in the shape
of a crown which identifies you as the rightful ruler
of the kingdom. ☐ **5 points**

You believe that reality TV is a waste of time that
eats up valuable hours of your life that could be
spent learning Klingon. ☐ **5 points**

You believe that the chances of machines taking
over from humans one day are about 50-50. ☐ **3 points**

You believe that the effects on *Blake's Seven*
were good for their day. ☐ **3 points**

You believe that Orson Welles' greatest
performance was as Unicron in
Transformers: The Movie. ☐ **3 points**

...and that *Super Mario Brothers* is the best
Bob Hoskins film. ☐ **3 points**

OPINIONS

...and that Spielberg's most poignant and moving exploration of Nazi Germany is *Indiana Jones and the Last Crusade*.

☐ 3 points

You believe that *The X-Files* was canceled because it was revealing too much, rather than because it had jumped the shark.

☐ 3 points

You believe that JFK, Princess Diana, Kurt Cobain, Biggie and Tupac were all assassinated by the FBI and the Freemasons because they knew too much.

☐ 5 points

You believe that the mobile phone tower at the gas station near your house was put there by the government, which is monitoring you.

☐ 5 points

After watching *The Truman Show*, you became convinced that you were the subject of a secret reality TV show, and all your actions were being watched by viewers around the world.

☐ 5 points

You get annoyed by people who think that the name of the film is always the name of the central character in the film too, and shout out things like "Go on, Die Hard!" and "Get him, Total Recall!"

☐ 2 points

You get annoyed by people who fall for obvious email hoaxes like the one about the person who does a good deed for an Arab and gets a tip-off about an imminent terrorist attack, and the one from the Nigerian millionaire who wants your bank account details.

☐ 2 points

You get annoyed by people who like a movie remake but haven't seen the original.

☐ 2 points

You get annoyed by people who buy computers from Best Buy rather than a proper computer shop.

☐ 3 points

ARE YOU A GEEK?

You get annoyed when rock or pop groups use punctuation as a design feature, as with the asterisk before *NSYNC and the umlauts heavy metal bands add to make themselves seem more Germanic and scary.

☐ **3 points**

You were disappointed when all the things that had been predicted for the year 2000, such as hover packs, food pills and moon holidays, failed to come true.

☐ **2 points**

You know that Greedo did not shoot first.

☐ **3 points**

...and that the police in *ET* did not have walkie-talkies in their hands.

☐ **3 points**

You've written an angry letter to a TV station when sporting events have interrupted regular programming.

☐ **1 point**

You've written an angry letter to a TV station when a sci-fi show has been canceled.

☐ **3 points**

You've written an angry letter to a TV station when one of their period dramas featured something that wasn't invented until a few years later.

☐ **5 points**

You've written an angry letter to the Booker Prize committee demanding to know why Alan Moore has never won.

☐ **3 points**

You have a favorite number.

☐ **1 point**

...it's pi.

☐ **3.1416 points**

...it's e.

☐ **2.7183 points**

It's the answer to the ultimate question of life, the universe and everything.

☐ **42 points**

You believe you've experienced a glitch in the matrix.

☐ 2 points

You believe the Segway is a brilliant invention that will soon eradicate forever the unnecessary hassle of walking.

☐ 3 points

You genuinely can't understand why *Tron* wasn't nominated for the best picture Oscar.

☐ 3 points

You genuinely can't understand why humans don't behave more like Vulcans.

☐ 4 points

You have an opinion about crop circles, spontaneous combustion, big cats and alien abduction.

☐ 1 point

You have an opinion about who would win in a fight between two fictional characters.

☐ 3 points

You've staged this fight using action figurines.

☐ 5 points

You've had an argument about whether the Spectrum 48K is better than the Commodore 64.

☐ 1 point

You've had this argument within the last year.

☐ 3 points

Your favorite smell is that of new comics.

☐ 2 points

You're not speaking to your friend until he admits that *Babylon 5* was better than *Star Trek*.

☐ 5 points

The first thing you do after you see a film you like is calculate where it stands in your top hundred films of the year.

☐ 4 points

You've glanced with disgust at someone on a train who's still using a personal CD player rather than an iPod.

☐ 3 points

You've had an argument about which genre a song should be classified under on an iPod.

☐ 3 points

ARE YOU A GEEK?

The type of pollution that annoys you most is light pollution, as this interferes with your stargazing. ☐ 2 points

You've had an argument with a small child because they said they preferred the Harry Potter books to *His Dark Materials*. ☐ 3 points

You've read the manifestos of all the political parties in their entirety when deciding how to cast your vote. ☐ 2 points

...and decided to tear up your ballot, as none of them mentioned the space program. ☐ 5 points

You get annoyed by people who only read books like *The Hitchhiker's Guide to the Galaxy* or *I, Robot* when they're released in movie tie-in editions. ☐ 4 points

List your top five films of all time below

1 . . . .

2 . . . .

3 . . . .

4 . . . .

5 . . . .

List your top five albums of all time below

1 . . . .

2 . . . .

3 . . . .

4 . . . .

5 . . . .

List your top five songs of all time below

1 ....

2 ....

3 ....

4 ....

5 ....

List your top five computer games of all time below

1 ....

2 ....

3 ....

4 ....

5 ....

List your top five novels of all time below

1 ....

2 ....

3 ....

4 ....

5 ....

Award yourself extra points if, while filling in the top five lists above, you

...wrote the lists without hesitation, because you've worked them all out before. ☐ 1 point

...avoided putting something in your top five lists because it was too much of an obvious choice, like *Sergeant Pepper's Lonely Hearts Club Band* or *The Lord of the Rings*. ☐ 1 point

ARE YOU A GEEK?

...**included** something because it's underrated,
rather than because you really like it. □ 1 point

...**included** something because it's not the sort of
thing people would expect you to like. □ 1 point

...**avoided** including anything made in
the last 10 years. □ 2 points

...**even in** the computer games section. □ 3 points

Total points for this section:

Total points so far:

• COMMUNICATION

SKILLS •

You've gone a whole day without speaking to anyone.

☐ 2 points

You've gone a whole week without speaking to anyone.

☐ 3 points

You've gone a whole month without speaking to anyone.

☐ 4 points

You've spent so much time on your own that you forgot what you were saying out loud and what you were just thinking inside your head.

☐ 5 points

You never make eye contact with anyone.

☐ 2 points

You sometimes forget to leave gaps in your conversation for the other person to talk.

☐ 2 points

You've continued a lengthy point you were making during a phone conversation after someone has said, "Okay, well I better be going now."

☐ 2 points

You often repeat the same point more than three times in an argument, as you assume that the person who's disputing it can't understand it.

☐ 3 points

You often pretend to feel more strongly about something than you actually do, for the sake of a good argument.

☐ 1 point

You have a lisp.

☐ 1 point

You've called someone in the middle of the night to tell them a point you forgot to make in an argument that you had earlier that day.

☐ 3 points

Your natural tone of voice is sarcasm.

☐ 2 points

You speak as if there is a full stop after every word in every sentence.

☐ 3 points

You often refer to things by their Latin names.

☐ 2 points

You've made a Latin pun.

☐ 4 points

When someone asks you how you are, you actually give them a detailed account of your current state of health.

☐ 2 points

•BONUS POINTS•

Your voice resembles that of:

Crispin Glover in Back to the Future

☐ 1 point

Emo Phillips

☐ 2 points

Gilbert Gottfried

☐ 3 points

Dustin Hoffman in Rain Man

☐ 4 points

A Speak & Spell machine

☐ 5 points

You've told someone that swearing is a sign of a limited vocabulary.

☐ 2 points

You've pointed out what the operative word in someone's sentence was.

☐ 2 points

YOUR HANDWRITING IS DISCONNECTED AND WIDELY SPACED, WHICH GRAPHOLOGISTS SEE AS A SIGN OF ANTISOCIAL TENDENCIES.

☐ 3 POINTS

You will always email rather than phone.

☐ 3 points

You have more than one email address (add a point for each additional one).

◯ points

You've inserted "(sic)" after a spelling mistake when forwarding an email.

☐ 1 point

You've organized your email address book into groups like "Pratchett nutters" and "*Red Dwarf* loonies."

☐ 3 points

You do not own an actual, physical address book.

☐ 5 points

You have a rule with your friends that the subject line of an email must always be a line from a film.

☐ 3 points

You were very perplexed when you had to send an actual, physical letter to your aunt who doesn't have email.

☐ 1 point

You've used the chat room acronym IRL, meaning "In Real Life," to describe things that are done away from computers.

☐ 5 points

You've tried to press Control-Alt-Delete, and then realized that it wasn't possible because you were IRL.

☐ 5 points

You've given an inappropriately philosophical answer to the question "Why are you doing that?"

☐ 3 points

ARE YOU A GEEK?

You've answered a question in an unnecessarily pedantic way. So, for example, when someone has asked you what your name is, you've said, "It's a word designated to me by my parents to make it easier to distinguish me from others."

3 points

You've made the "over-your-head" gesture by swiping your hand over your head and making a swooshing noise.

2 points

You've made this hand gesture.

2 points

You've used the word "affirmative" instead of "yes."

2 points

You've used the word "ixnay" instead of "no."

3 points

You've used the phrase "ipso facto."

3 points

You've used the word "ergo."

3 points

You've used the phrase "de facto."

3 points

You've used the phrase "a priori."

3 points

You've used the word "perchance."

3 points

You've called someone an "ignoramus."

3 points

You've used the word "methinks."

3 points

You've used the word "perusal."

3 points

You've referred to a piece of jewelry as an "amulet."

3 points

You've said " 'scuse I" instead of "excuse me." □ 3 points

You've said "Fact!" after relating a fact to someone. □ 3 points

You've referred to some binoculars as "binos." □ 3 points

You've said "touché" after someone has made a good point in an argument. □ 3 points

You've said "QED" after winning an argument. □ 3 points

You've said "I rest my case, m'lord" after winning an argument. □ 5 points

You've stayed in character by using phrases like "verily," "forsooth" and "wench" during a role-playing game. □ 5 points

You often say "Not" after a sentence, in case people fail to pick up on your subtle sarcasm, as in "Last night's episode of *Voyager* was good. Not." □ 3 points

When someone was being hypocritical, you've said, "I believe the words 'pot,' 'kettle' and 'black' spring to mind." □ 3 points

---

•BONUS POINTS•

You always sign off your emails with the following:

So long, and thanks for all the fish □ 1 point

Be seeing you □ 3 points

Live long and prosper □ 5 points

[124] 1111100

ARE YOU A GEEK?

You've used the following emoticons in emails:

:-) ☐ 1 point

:-(☐ 3 points

;-) ☐ 5 points

You've said, "I stand corrected." ☐ 2 points

You've asked a barman for a pint of his "finest mead." ☐ 3 points

You've asked a barman for "real ale: a pint thereof." ☐ 5 points

You've used the phrase "Very interesting, Mr. Bond" when playing a board game. ☐ 3 points

You've said "Me three," after someone has said, "Me too." ☐ 4 points

You've added a phrase like "he said, knowingly" to the end of a sentence. ☐ 5 points

You've said "open brackets" and "close brackets" in conversation to make the syntax of your sentence clear. ☐ 3 points

When one of your friends has made a stupid point in an argument, you've said, "Earth calling [name of your friend]." ☐ 3 points

You've said "There is a God!" upon seeing a picture of a seminaked woman. ☐ 3 points

When asking someone to explain themselves, you've said, "Care to expand on the why?" ☐ 3 points

COMMUNICATION SKILLS

When making points in conversation, you list them a, b, c, d, and so on. ⬜ 2 points

You've used the phrase "quote unquote." ⬜ 2 points

...and emphasized it with the finger quotes gesture. ⬜ 5 points

You've referred to a fantasy author as a "sculptor of dreams." ⬜ 5 points

You've said, "I have a bad feeling about this." ⬜ 2 points

You've said, "The Force is strong in this one" while choosing vegetables in the supermarket. ⬜ 3 points

You've said, "I cannae change the laws of physics, Captain" while driving. ⬜ 4 points

You've said, "I will not be pushed, filed, stamped, indexed, briefed, debriefed or numbered. My life is my own," while on the phone to your bank. ⬜ 5 points

You've used an abbreviation for a movie or TV show, like ID4, T3 or LXG. ⬜ 1 point

---

•BONUS POINTS•

You refuse to use familiar contractions for the following:

Telephone ⬜ 1 point

Perambulator ⬜ 3 points

Omnibus ⬜ 5 points

ARE YOU A GEEK?

When angry with someone, you've said, "Please arrange the following words into a well-known phrase: 'off' and 'piss'."

☐ 4 points

You've used the phrase, "I think you're confusing me with someone who actually gives a shit."

☐ 3 points

You've said "No shit, Sherlock" to someone who has just stated the obvious.

☐ 3 points

You've said "Your powers of deduction are staggering" to someone who has just stated the obvious.

☐ 5 points

You've used the acronym FYI in an email.

☐ 2 points

You've used the acronym FYI in a conversation.

☐ 3 points

Next time you meet up with your friends, take this Geek Bingo card with you. Cross out a word whenever it's said, and award yourself three points for a full row and five points for a full house.

◯ points

ergo	premise	affirmative	life-form	regenerate
myriad	verily	peruse	surmise	quote
matrices	fractal	Free Square	ipso facto	to wit
empirical	FAQ	extrapolate	server	unquote
continuum	vortices	thereof	forsooth	methinks

You've used the acronym IMHO. ☐ 2 points

You've used the acronym BTW. ☐ 2 points

You've used the acronym TMI. ☐ 2 points

You've used the acronym BRB. ☐ 2 points

You've used the acronym RTFM. ☐ 3 points

You've used the acronym WYSIWYG. ☐ 4 points

You've used the acronym EOD. ☐ 5 points

You've used the phrase "clinically insane" to
describe a slightly more extroverted friend. ☐ 5 points

Total points for this section:

Total points so far:

ARE YOU A GEEK?

Total scores

Total points for "Lifestyle" section: ....

Total points for "Style" section: ....

Total points for "Social Life" section: ....

Total points for "Entertainment" section: ....

Total points for "Hobbies" section: ....

Total points for "Sex" section: ....

Total points for "Intelligence" section: ....

Total points for "Knowledge" section: ....

Total points for "Childhood" section: ....

Total points for "Opinions" section: ....

Total points for "Communication Skills" section: ....

Total Points:

Now draw a pie chart representing the breakdown of your total score by section, and complete one of the certificates on the following pages.

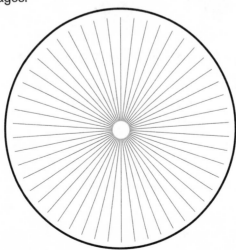

This is to certify that

. . . .

scored less than 300 geek points,

and is officially

not a geek

It is safe to speak to

this person.

This is to certify that

· ·

scored between

300 and 1000 geek points, and

officially qualifies as a

geek

It is safe to speak to this person,

but you should not try to make

eye contact with them.

This is to certify that

. . . .

scored between 1001 and 1500

geek points, and officially

qualifies as an

übergeek

Please only use email to

communicate with this

person, except in emergency

circumstances.

This is to certify that

. . . .

scored between 1501 and 2000 geek points, and officially qualifies as a

nerd

It is only possible to communicate with this person by email.

This is to certify that

. . . .

scored over 2000 geek points,

and officially qualifies as a

nerdmeister general

You are not advised to

communicate with this person

under any circumstances.

HOW DID YOU SCORE?

If your geek score was higher than you expected, don't worry. Rather than trying to hide or change your behavior, why not embrace and accept your geekiness? You could hold a "coming out" party in which you explain to your family and friends that being a geek is your lifestyle choice and they should accept it. Or, better still, you could arrange a "coming out" party but then stay in your room and refuse to come downstairs when everyone turns up.

Here are a few things you can use when you're "coming out":

10 PRINT "I'M
    A GEEK AND
    I'M NOT
    ASHAMED"
20 GO TO 10

PLACARD

SAY IT LOUD!
I'M A GEEK
AND I'M PROUD!

T-SHIRT

GEEK

BADGE

FYI

Things you really should have known while reading this book.

Lifestyle

1138 is a popular geek number because of the George Lucas film *THX 1138*. You can access an Easter egg on the DVD of *The Phantom Menace* by selecting the "Language Selection" menu on disc one, highlighting the THX logo in the corner, typing in "1138" on your remote and pressing "enter."

Entertainment

To see *Dark Side of the Moon* spookily matching *The Wizard of Oz,* press "play" on your CD player when the MGM lion roars for the third time.

"Pan and Scan" refers to the method of cropping the sides off a widescreen film to show it on old-fashioned TV.

Examples of rubbish sequels are *The Matrix: Reloaded, Highlander 2: The Quickening* and *Batman and Robin. The Phantom Menace* does not count, as it is a prequel. And the pod race bit is quite good.

An Easter egg is a hidden feature on a DVD or computer game.

The "ghost" that appears in *Three Men and a Baby* is actually a cardboard cutout of Ted Danson that was left on the set by mistake.

There is no on-screen Munchkin suicide in *The Wizard of Oz.*

The third Stormtrooper that enters the control room where R2-D2 and C-3PO are hiding is the one who bangs his head in *Star Wars.* Or *Episode Four* or *A New Hope* or whatever you call it.

You can see the word "Sex" in *The Lion King* in the scene where Simba, Timon and Pumba are lying on the edge of a cliff. Simba walks to the edge of the cliff and lies down on the ground, causing a cloud of dust to spell out the word.

The footage of Brandon Lee being fatally wounded was not used in *The Crow.*

Hobbies

A blog, or weblog, is a diary that's been posted online.

Sex

The abbreviations ST:TOS, ST:TNG, ST:DS9, ST:VOY and ST:ENT refer to the various incarnations of *Star Trek: The Original Series, The Next Generation, Deep Space Nine, Voyager* and *Enterprise.*

Intelligence

"Hexadecimal" refers to the base 16 number system.

You've found a "Googlewhack" if you type two words into Google and get a single search result, as detailed on googlewhack.com and in *Dave Gorman's Googlewhack Adventure* from Ebury Press.

The reason why three buses always come along at once is this: even if all the buses leave the depot at equal intervals, as soon as one bus suffers any kind of

ARE YOU A GEEK?